LOSERS, LIARS & LEECHES

Losers, Liars & Leeches
True Stories of a Slumlord

Max Bumgardner

Copyright 2020 © by Max Bumgardner
All rights reserved.

Believing you're a good person and actually being one are two completely different things.
—Anonymous

Contents

Introduction ix

Mariah's Story: The Painful Price of Immaturity 1

Bonnie and the Thug 13

Up the Neighbor's Asses 27

You Can't Take My Front Door Off 38

We Found Ants and Spiders: We're Suing 52

Do You Take Gift Cards for Rent? 63

The Wisdom of Perseverance 74

Sorry, Ms. Jackson, I Ain't No Fool 83

Walking from Helter-Shelter 92

Drunken Dementia 102

Conclusion 112

Blessings Along the Way 128

Advice for Tenants and Landlords 133

About the Author 136

Introduction

Thank you for purchasing this book.

My heart has hardened as a result of being a landlord. I believe that there are some really lazy, self-centered people among us that pose as victims and are anything but.

Let me be really clear about a couple of things. First I did it wrong. All of it. I rushed into it and then tried to play hero. I was in way over my head and didn't run it like a business. I became emotionally involved in many cases, and that too was a mistake, quickly sinking me into trouble. We all have different thresholds on what we can handle. I found out my limit fairly quickly.

Second there is nothing wrong with being poor. Being poor doesn't equate to being a worthless human being. You can be a billionaire and be a total shithead, right? Turn on the news if you need proof. Some of my favorite people in the world had nothing. One was my great-grandfather who spent his entire life helping others in need. Whether it was a roof over someone's head for the night or a hot meal at dinner time, he and his lifelong partner, his wife, provided whatever was needed. He watched his wife slip away inch by inch on a rented hospital bed in the living room of their tiny mobile home on the Mississippi River in Iowa. He had nothing but love and service in his heart all the days of his life. He wouldn't think of a handout. As a boy my great-grandfather, along with two of his brothers, slept under a bear skin in a cabin. They didn't have shit. Nothing. He worked into his eighties and was thankful for the meager pay he received. He had the type of character that is missing in so many today. I don't share his level of compassion, so I don't measure up with him. You will see that in the pages to follow.

Being a landlord is a miserable experience unless you have buckets of money and a large team of people that are strategically layered between you and your tenants. I made the mistake of plunging in without thinking it all the way through beforehand. Being accessible to my tenants and getting emotionally involved in their lives took a huge toll on my family. I believed their pathetic stories of struggle even when it was almost always self-imposed. I did that because as a child I spent time in government housing, owing to an alcoholic, abusive, skirt-chasing, uneducated father. My mother took us, leaving him and the house, to save us. She was without resources or education. So in our case, low-income housing was a life saver. We used it as it was intended to be used.

I remember the smell of the fresh paint in the two-bedroom townhouse my mother moved my younger brother and me into back in the 1970s. I was so relieved that we would have a place of our own and I wouldn't have to sleep on my grandparents' couch anymore, as I had done the previous six months. Nor would I have to worry about my father coming home in the middle of the night to beat the shit out of my mother in an alcohol-fueled rage. That low-income townhouse represented refuge and a new start—an experience and discovery which would burrow its way into my impressionable soul. I loved it at the time. I was happy and grateful to be there, a ten-year-old "housing kid" and proud of it.

Fast forward thirty years and, apparently, I was virtue signaling to the world that I was something special—a legend in my own mind. I was returning to the hood to pull up others. I started purchasing run-down structures that were inhabited by the lowest among us. *These are my people*, I thought, as I toured the units before purchasing them. I was thinking a new kitchen there, a new roof here, some new windows on this one, maybe a playground for the kids at this place, and so on. I was a dreamer. More appropriately, a dumb ass. What I didn't know hit me like a freight train and almost took away everything that was most important to me, including my wife and kids. I was blinded by my own ignorance. I didn't do the hard work up front to thoroughly check some of these lowlifes out before helping them with a place to live.

I purchased all the "make money in real estate" courses. I had the books, the cassettes, the old VCR tapes, the seminars on DVDs. I devoured all of it and fully intended on putting my kids through college, as well as funding my own retirement. My plan was to purchase distressed properties with creative financing and then do the work myself. It seemed almost too easy. I was consuming program material made by people who were great at making program material. What I never found out was if these "experts" had ever actually accomplished in the real world what they were teaching. There wasn't an emotional intelligence component in any of the material I was consuming. Google reviews weren't as popular and telling as they are now. Plus, why mess with due diligence when the money is cheap? It was 2007 and the economy was roaring, right? I could keep purchasing, keep borrowing, keep helping. DUMB ASS!

At the height of my investment property empire, I had fifteen units, comprising a mix of single-family houses and apartment buildings. That isn't much compared with many serious real estate investor portfolios, but it was my whole world for a time—that is, for ten savage years. I was working a full-time job and operating a seasonal restaurant business in a state park. And most important—I had a beautiful wife and two adorable young kids at home. Instead of spending time with the three of them, I would typically be dealing with the tenants and their truckload of idiotic setbacks that they had created for themselves. So when I did get home at the end of a stress-filled day, I brought angst and rage with me. The effects of which helped shape parts of my relationships with loved ones to this day, and that was my fault too. Being a landlord for these sorry sad sacks changed my soul. What started as a mission to give back turned into hatred toward others in general. My kids are now adults. The rentals have all been sold. But thoughts of the time and money spent—time and money I will never get back—still sting today.

My biggest problem going in was that I was undercapitalized. To do what I wanted to do would have taken several hundred thousand dollars. The second biggest problem was that I didn't have any help—I never asked for it. Plus, I was a sucker for hard-luck stories. Those three ingredients combined resulted in failure.

The moment any landlord tries to reason with a tenant on an emotional level is the moment they give away their power. It's all downhill from there. While it's great to show other humans compassion in their time of need, there needs to be established, reasonable boundaries. It's also a mistake to extend courtesy via your bank account without requiring some accountability. Especially if you can't afford to lose what you are offering to someone. Very rarely were the problems with the tenants a result of random circumstance, such as a debilitating illness or an accident. In nearly every case their problems stemmed from a lack of education and from laziness, addiction, and zero accountability for colossally bad decisions.

Being a landlord sucked. I hated it and it wasn't about the clogged toilets at 3 a.m.—I didn't deal with those, ever. My lease stated that I didn't unclog toilets. (The only exception to that was when there was a tree root in a sewage line that was causing a total backup into the home instead of the toilet.) Typically, when I talked about my portfolio of houses, people would say that they would never be a landlord because of "clogged toilets in the middle of the night." In my experience that wasn't ever an issue. It was the *people* that I couldn't stand. The lying, cheating, self-absorbed people that I nearly let ruin my life. The toilets weren't nearly as full of shit as the people were.

Maybe I was too young to notice when I was living in government housing as a child that the people in that housing community were there because of their own choices. I still believe in government assistance because bad things happen and sometimes people need help. The problem I have is with the people abusing the program who end up breeding generations of takers. Why is it acceptable for someone who is capable, to do nothing and live for free? There are job opportunities everywhere today. There were plentiful jobs when I was a landlord. So I never understood the freeloaders and why it was acceptable for those same people to destroy property that wasn't theirs to destroy. I thought I was one of them originally, right? But I wasn't at all. What separated us was character.

As a landlord my primary competitor was the government. My mistake here was not taking this competitor seriously. The people running housing-authority agencies were not my allies. They work for the government with the goal of getting what they can for their client instead of helping them get back on their feet and be self-sufficient. Currently they are building more housing in my region. One entire housing complex was torn down so they could provide central air conditioning instead of window units to the tenants. That is a true story. Brand new places for people to live. How is a landlord of low-income housing supposed to compete with that? Yes, I believe everyone in our society deserves a clean place to live. But brand new houses? Where did this get so grossly off track? When did we stop requiring people to take care of their own? When did we send the message that it's OK to keep having children that you can't support? My own mother needed help in '70s and I am better for having received it. She never intended to stay there and didn't; we knew it was temporary the day we moved in. But that mindset of *temporary assistance* has been distorted and is now somehow a right—a right to a new house, a right to free rent—and it's all bullshit.

Government housing was only part of the problem. Another mistake I made was not properly assessing the competition from major real estate corporations that built low-income housing based on tax incentives and government-backed loans. Those companies as well have unlimited resources at their disposal.

Simultaneously competing with the government and large corporations should have been enough for any reasonable person to back away. But it never crossed my mind. Instead, I bought old, shitty units that needed everything and were in equally shitty parts of town. Plus I overpaid, without running the numbers for different scenarios. When I started I had a relatively low debt, a high income, and a chunk of money in the bank.

Having lived in government-subsidized housing for a time as a child, I genuinely thought I could help people and turn some lives around as I did my own. I discounted the fact that many of the residents in low-income housing choose to be there. It's not that they are *unable* to do things differently; it's that they *refuse* to do things differently. They are comfortable living for free. Why wouldn't they be? We make it too damn easy. No, that's not everyone. No, that's not a certain ethnicity. And no, I am not talking about the mentally or physically impaired either. The group that I am talking about is the low-life, instant-gratification freaks that have an overwhelming sense of entitlement and spend their days staring into a screen looking for their next opportunity "to take." The type of person that never puts a single thing back into the bucket. They don't do anything for anyone else because they are too focused on themselves.

Another mistake I made was to compare some of these single mothers to my own mother or my own wife. Growing up we always had a clean place to live, plenty to eat, and enough clothing to get by. My mother was a divorcée who worked a minimum wage job for most of her life. She never made much money but she always maximized what she had. She sacrificed for us boys and made sure our primary needs were met. I compared my mother to some of the mothers I encountered. One thing became abundantly clear in a hurry: my mom was a decent human being, and many of these women were not. Many of these women kept having kids that they couldn't support. They didn't clean their homes, themselves, or their children. They smoked, drank, did drugs, lived in filth, and didn't work or go to school. They were master manipulators masquerading as women of character, such as my own mother or wife.

I believed that because some of my favorite people growing up were low-income, I was jumping into a rewarding experience filled with life lessons on character and sacrifice. I believed that I could be the bridge to a better life for others by offering opportunities. I was wrong. The majority were shitty people, plain and simple. Self-centered assholes that went from handout to handout without ever taking any personal responsibility. It wasn't their fault that I almost lost it all. It was mine. I know that now.

I fell for the stories of hardship and bad breaks. I believed it when they said they would be different by taking care of the property, by paying their rent on time, by not causing any problems. Most were total liars. They were dirtbags who in many cases were scamming the government and me at the same time.

My problem with being a landlord was with the people. People who make horrible decisions and then want to place the blame elsewhere. The low-income tenants were getting worse too. Smart phones and dumb people aren't a good match.

Being a low-income-housing landlord isn't about collecting checks—unless you keep it about collecting checks and make it all business. I made the mistake of being kind. For me it was about being a father, a brother, a preacher, a banker, a friend, an enemy, a maintenance man, a bill collector, a judge, a janitor, a taxi, a security guard, a mediator, a private investigator, a pawn shop, a trash dump, and an enforcer.

I hope my experiences can save someone else the agony of dealing with deadbeats disguised as human beings who need a chance. I believe in grace. We need to help our brothers and sisters. But where do you draw the line with drug addicts masked as responsible citizens? Or with pathological liars veiled as honest, hardworking people? For me it was too much. It had to come to an end. The Bible says to forgive "seventy times seven." So by that measuring stick, I failed. I struggled with it too. Did I owe all these people endless chances while I was ruining my own life financially and otherwise? It was time, I concluded, to put it down. I figured the government agencies could handle it. I support those agencies too by paying taxes (I have worked since age twelve).

The deals were not complicated because most investment property owners will gladly sell their problems to the next sucker that comes along. The maintenance horror stories aren't as horrible as most believe them to be. It's the people. It's the fucking people.

In the coming chapters, you will read stories that will seem made up or embellished. They are not. Only the names have been changed to protect their sorry asses. I don't wish anything bad on the people portrayed in the pages that follow. In fact, initially I saw something good in each of them or I wouldn't have rented to them. My hope is that the good in them takes over and that they get their lives on track.

The day I decided to write this book is the day that I watched a scumbag unwrap a hamburger on the front steps of the unit he was staying. He wasn't on the lease, mind you, so I didn't even know his name. Rather than use the wrapper to eat the burger, and then throw it away, this moron let the wrapper and sack drop on the ground as he walked to the bus stop. I had visions of running at him full speed, tackling him to the ground, and beating the shit out of him. That's not healthy. I knew I was near the end of my career as a landlord.

I didn't know at the time when I signed the loan documents that I would end up cleaning feces, urine, blood, vomit, skin, used condoms, dead animal carcasses, rotten food, sullied diapers, piles of dirty laundry, and bags and bags of garbage that never made it the few steps to the dumpster. I didn't know that one winter I would be doing an army crawl in sewage water under a house, so I could clean out a sewer line that some idiot woman kept flushing tampons down. And on, and on, and on.

I did not do it right at all and ultimately deserved what I got. All I can say is that I was trying to help people the whole time. *That* was my intention. Help people while building a financial cushion for my family. I am so glad I got out of the business and let it all go. My life was instantly better the day the last unit was gone. An amazing relief.

I firmly believe some people need to wallow in their own shit for years and decide whether they want to take responsibility for their life—or continue to be pathetic. My heart aches for the children of these sorry people.

Ultimately, it is none of my business; I don't have to be a part of the problematic, self-defeating decisions these people make.

If someone offered me their entire low-income portfolio for free at this point, I would turn it down. There is no way. And remember, if you can't get it dirt cheap or free, don't even think about it because it's not worth it. The government is the king of low-income property. They will build brand new housing for some of your worst tenants and let them live there free.

The most critical step for success in the rental property business is for you to *select your tenants wisely*. If you diligently do this work on the front end, you will always benefit. Eliminating bad tenants upfront means that you can spend your time on your business instead of someone else's problems. Don't make exceptions, ever.

What follows are a few stories to dissuade you from purchasing low-income properties. If you are going to purchase investment property, I recommend you purchase nice properties—stay out of the low-income rental space altogether. It's simply not worth it.

At the start of each chapter, I will highlight tips both for tenants and for landlords. As you work your way through the chapters, you may begin to notice that some bullet points are applicable to more than one chapter. That is because many tenants, as you will soon discover, committed the same transgressions.

Mariah's Story
The Painful Price of Immaturity

<u>For Tenants</u>

- Never assume that your being homeless is somehow the   landlord's problem.
- Don't ever let anyone else live with you that is not on the lease.
- Call the landlord during *regular business hours,* and be respectful.

<u>For Landlords</u>

- If this is a young person's first time renting, steer clear unless you can get their parent or a cosigner to shoulder responsibility. Make no exceptions.
- If the rent is late and you can't reach the renter, don't waste *any* time. Call the guarantor(s) and let them know you are having problems. Let them know the associated late fees and the terms of the lease make it their problem too.
- Don't let tenants call you at all hours of the day and night. In writing, present your established office hours to renters. Make it clear that you will not answer the phone after a specific time of day unless

it is an emergency. Make clear to them what constitutes an emergency. No exceptions.

With tears running down her face, she said, "Can you work with me?" Mariah was standing in front of a two-bedroom house that I owned, holding hands with an adorable little girl, so cute and innocent, and fatherless. With no place of their own, mother and daughter had been bouncing from house to house. I wanted to help that little girl so badly. She was only four. I thought about what it would be like if my little girl were in the same situation. Would someone help her?

The girl said, "Mommy, can we live here? I love this house."

The house was old and in a run-down part of town, situated right behind a car lot.

"I get paid next week, and I can bring you the deposit then. I have fifty right now. I won't have all the rent for another two weeks though."

I was about to make a walloping mistake that would cost me thousands: I did work with her. I held the unit and let them move in without my receiving the first month's rent. With only the deposit money in hand, I was taking a huge chance.

When my parents divorced, my father moved not only two hookers into our family home but also a local bar owner. My father was out having sex, drinking, and partying. My mother, brother, and I were staying with my grandparents. We didn't have anywhere else to go. For half a year my bed was my grandparent's couch, while my mother saved enough to put down a deposit for a unit in a government-assisted housing complex.

I was comparing Mariah to my mother. But Mariah was someone else entirely. She was someone's problem—the daughter who hadn't yet grown up herself. She was a lazy, dirty, manipulative liar. The only thing she did have in common with my mother was that she was a mother herself.

Mariah brought in a thug boyfriend almost immediately. She knew that the lease stated she and her daughter were the *only* tenants, and she knew what that meant. She looked right into my eyes and promised that there wouldn't be anyone else living in the house. She didn't mention that she would be bringing in a recently released drug convict. He moved in within days of her receiving the keys. He and all his nasty thug friends had an all-night party at the house, disrupting the entire neighborhood in the first week. Consequently, I received calls from neighbors and the police. I didn't even know this guy's name.

About the same time the wild thug party took place, Mariah informed me via text that she was unemployed. She stated that the rent she had promised would be late and that she was going to file for unemployment benefits. I found out she was fired for not showing up to work. She didn't call or anything. She just quit showing up, and in her mind, she qualified for unemployment.

Mariah had called me multiple times within her first three weeks of living in the house. On one occasion, she exclaimed, "Deez blinds ugly. When are you gonna do something 'bout dem?"

I was waiting for her to laugh or say she was kidding. She wasn't. She had changed her talk track to that of a gangsta! I was amazed at how quickly she could be someone so incredibly different once she knew she had her hooks in. I could hear the confidence in her voice.

She was calling me at about 11:30 p.m. to tell me the blinds needed to be replaced and I needed to do something about them. I explained that she was welcome to purchase some new window coverings and that the Dollar Store down the street sold them for seven bucks.

"I ain't got no time to put up no damn blinds." Click.

I went back to sleep.

In Mariah's short life of twenty-two years, everything had been provided. When she was hungry, she walked to the refrigerator. When she was cold, she turned up the furnace. When she was tired, she took a nap. Mariah expected *me* to replace the blinds. But I didn't replace window coverings—that was the *tenant's* responsibility. It was in the lease—the lease she had never read.

The next call from Mariah went like this: "You need to call yo' plumber. There be fuckin' water all over the floor in the baffroom."

Keep in mind, there were never any pleasantries exchanged—such as, *How are you doing?* or *Sorry to bother you; I just had a quick question.* Nope, with her trashy wannabe-gangsta ass, it was straight to attack mode, as if she were the queen of the universe, and I her lowly servant.

I tried to find out what the source of the water on the floor was.

She said, "How am I 'pose to know? Fuckin' water on the floor, and it ain't 'pose to be dere. I'm sick of dis shit. You need to get yo' plumber over here, too-day." Click.

Imagine dealing with someone like this, who hadn't paid you all of what they said they would. Then imagine knowing it's your own fault, and now you are in it knee-deep. All because you were acting from your heart instead of conducting business. You were trying to help a cute four-year-old girl have a roof over her head. Very noble thoughts that were unrealistic because of the train-wreck-moron-of-a-mother Mariah was. The same person that promised she only needed a chance, tears welling in her eyes as she stood in the driveway less than a month prior. The same person that could speak in plain English and be respectful, while her adorable daughter looked on. That same person that was going to cost my family peace and thousands of dollars before she was done.

I left my job and drove over to the house to inspect the water on the bathroom floor. By this time I had chewed through my savings and was nearing my credit limits. Was it going to be several hundred, or several thousand? What could it be? I was always incredibly responsive to my tenants, and looking back, that too was a huge mistake.

When I arrived, I checked the water supply lines to the tub, the toilet, and the sinks. There wasn't water on the floor as she had indicated. No water coming from any of those places, in fact. I looked under the house in the crawl space—nothing and no evidence of water. I went back into the house and checked again, putting my hands on the floor behind the toilet to see if I could feel anything wet. Nothing. I was irritated. Then it hit me. As I looked up from the dirty bathroom floor—which I had just installed before Mariah moved in, the same floor that had taken a weekend to install—I noticed that there was no shower curtain.

"Mariah, are you all taking showers or baths?"

She confirmed that they were showering. I asked her where her shower curtain was.

She said, "We just lean to the leff."

I was pissed. I gave this lazy, entitled brat part of my day because I was worried about the unit and their safety. There was no problem other than they needed a damn shower curtain. I went to the Dollar Store and spent the fourteen dollars for a rod, some rings, and the curtain, then went back and installed them. The new vinyl from the shower curtain made the bathroom smell better. She just stared at the television, which was sitting on the floor in the smoke-filled living room, the whole time I was there.

Her little girl was somewhere else in the house, and her thug boyfriend was lying against the wall on a blow-up mattress, fixated on his phone. The screen's glow illuminated his scowling face, framed by his hoodie. I hoped that this would be the last time I'd heard from Ms. Mariah, but I knew it wouldn't. I could feel how it was going to get much, much worse.

A week later the phone rang again, around lunch time, which is when they got up for the day. I answered.

"It's mutha fuckin' hot in here. Air conditioner broke. When you gonna come and fix it?"

I asked her if she could turn the air conditioner on.

"Yeah, da mutha fucka on, but it still hot in here." Click.

I left my job, once again, and drove over to investigate. I knocked on the front door. When it finally opened the stench nearly knocked me out. The smell of body odor, cigarette smoke, fried food, and rotten garbage took over. And yes, it was mutha fuckin' hot inside.

"No smoking" is on the lease.

"No tenants other than those listed" is on the lease.

"No blankets or sheets as window covers" is on the lease.

"No nailing into wood or altering the appearance without express written permission" is on the lease.

No one cared about the lease, except for me.

There was no natural light inside because they had covered the windows with sheets and blankets, which they had nailed to the window trim. So it was fairly dark inside. And as always, a layer of smoke settled in the room. The little girl wasn't there. The thug boyfriend was staring at *Judge Judy* on the television, which sat on the floor with the power cord stretched as tightly as it would go, so he could have the TV in front of him where he sat. He didn't look up. He was a worthless thug looking for problems.

Mariah, with her bloated, stinky body, was sprawled out on the air mattress that occupied the center of the living room floor. The window air conditioning unit she was referring to was in this room.

"See, I told you it was fuckin' hot in here," she said, with a mean scowl on her face.

The front of the new air conditioner, which I had paid $450 for a month before, was ripped off and lying on the floor in pieces. The unit was running, but the air coming out of it was warm. The LED thermostat read eighty-four degrees. Next to the thermostat readout were two little arrows: one pointing up, one pointing down. I asked Mariah if she had already tried to adjust the thermostat.

"No, why I gotta fuck wit it?"

With each touch on the down arrow, we watched the number decrease—*84, 83, 82.*

"Mariah, this is what you have to do to adjust the temperature. What would you like it set at?"

"I want it cold in here."

I set the thermostat to sixty-nine degrees. We heard the compressor kick on and started to feel the cold air rushing out.

Before I left, I asked her if she was going to have rent on the first, which was days away.

"Yeah, I'll have it. I'll call you and tell you when you can come to get it, if I am home."

Not, *Yes, I will make sure you get it. Would you like me to bring it to you or mail it?*

No, it wasn't that way because she was a nasty entitled brat that hadn't ever grown up or taken any responsibility for anything to this point in her life.

As expected, Mariah didn't answer text messages on the 1st, the 2nd, or even the 3rd. She didn't answer phone calls or return messages. She didn't answer her door.

Finally, I lost my patience and sent her a text that read *Pay your rent or get your shit out of my house. I will gladly evict you if you would like me to do that. You have broken the lease many times over, and you are a total pain in the ass to deal with.*

I had never spoken a cross word to her up to this point. I had always been respectful and professional. Something in me cracked, and the compassion I had was replaced with unbridled rage.

Right after sending that text, I got a call from a number that was out of the area. I answered.

"Mutha fucka, don't you talk to my wife like that. Who you think you are sending shit like that on the phone? If you were a man, you'd come back and say that to my face, bitch."

I told him I would be right there and did a U-turn on the road. I probably could have killed innocent people driving because I was temporarily out of my mind. My hands were shaking. I was screaming in my car. "This piece of shit, lowlife wannabe thug is going to challenge me!"

He wasn't on the lease. He didn't have a job. He wasn't married to Mariah or to anyone, and he had never even introduced himself. He was a freeloading piece of shit in my house, who had been putting cigarettes out on the wood floor. Fuck him! I had had enough and was ready to roll.

Once I arrived, I got out of the car and went to pound on the door. I was out of control. He came outside and immediately changed his tune. He was a massive young man that could have easily overpowered me and done severe damage, but he didn't. Thank God.

He stuck his hand out to shake mine and said, "We ain't trying to cause problems. You don't need to be so mean to us."

Mean as in demanding the rent? Huh? I explained that he wasn't on the lease, that they hadn't returned calls, and that I had had enough. I told him to tell Mariah that I was quite serious about reaching my limit. No more drama; no more late rent; no more late-night parties outside; no more nasty phone calls. The next time it would be all over with, and they'd all be out on the street where they belonged until they could learn some respect.

Ultimately, she didn't pay. In my state, evicting someone is a process. The tenant gets a notice that is required by law, giving them some time. I pounded on the door. Once Mariah answered, I handed her the eviction notice, without an explanation, and got back in my car. She stood there in the doorway, holding it, trying to comprehend what had just happened. It was around noon and I knew she wasn't even awake yet, but I was in accordance with the law.

My phone rang about an hour later. This time it was a local number that I didn't recognize.

"Mr. Max, this is Melvin. I am Mariah's father. I want to talk with you about the hardship my daughter is going through and ask if you would work with her. Is there any way you could come and meet with my wife and me at our home? It would be a blessing to our family if you could make an exception, sir."

I went to their home reluctantly, burning another lunch hour and stealing time from my employer. It was in a sad part of town. I was hoping that they were going to write out a check for their precious little welfare princess, and I could go back to my stressed out, maxed out, angst ridden life.

I was met at the door by a huge man. He had a giant smile and extended his hand to shake mine.

"God bless you for coming to meet with us," he said.

We were all seated at a nice big table. The house was clean and orderly, with pictures of Jesus hanging on the wall. He explained that Mariah had had a difficult life and that if I could work with her a bit more, they were confident the good Lord was going to work it all out. He and his wife asked me to join their hands and pray with them on Mariah's behalf. I did. Looking back now, I fully understand that these people didn't want her back at their house, even if that is what Jesus wanted. The monster they had created was more than they could handle, and they were eager to pray the problem off on me. Shame on them.

Her father shared that they were on a fixed income and living in government-subsidized housing because of their disabilities—disabilities that were not easy to spot, given their mobility appeared perfect. So for at least two generations, paying for your own home was considered optional. I was now aware of where Mariah's sense of entitlement came from, and the resentment grew.

Plus, her father wasn't her father at all. He was a guy that her mother was living with, so they could run their own little game. They too were scamming the system by combining vouchers for food and housing that were supposed to be for two separate households. They revealed that to me in our conversation, inadvertently, just before we joined hands to pray. They had different names and were pooling their entitlement benefits together to maximize them. The agencies that were paying would call it *fraud*, not a blessing.

I never got the rent. The notice expired, and I received a court date with my attorney, as well as an order to vacate from a judge. Then I had to wait an additional period before I could take possession of the property. Once that time passed, I had to remove a whole house full of contents that Mariah was not coming back to get. She trashed it all. Walls, doors, flooring, light fixtures, and ceilings—I replaced. It was unbelievable how much damage she did in just four months. All while paying zero rent.

The shocking part of the story happened some six months after I bounced Mariah back into the universe. She called me wanting to apologize and inquired about getting the same house back.

"That was a beautiful house and you really took care of it."

I told her it wasn't available. Then she asked if I had any other units available because she had just been evicted. I explained that I would never help her again and that she needed to treat people with respect. I told her never to call me for any reason moving forward. I ended the call and blocked her number. By the way, she was speaking Standard English. She wasn't the gangsta rappa queen she had been when totally destroying my house. She was able to switch back to a respectable human being, momentarily, when she needed help. Crazy how that works, isn't it?

Mariah ended up costing me about $6,000 and a bunch of time, between the lost rent, the court costs, and the damage to the home. Plus, we had to dispose all her belongings. She also clogged the toilet and left a huge pile of feces in the bathroom for me to deal with. That was her final goodbye.

Bonnie and the Thug

For Tenants

- You don't get to spend the landlord's money on remodeling the unit. If you don't like the way the rental unit looks when you go to view it, you shouldn't rent it.
- Letting guests stay at your home for more than ten business days is *not* allowed. It could cost you an eviction; the eviction could cost you your housing voucher, if you rely on one.
- Calling emergency services is only necessary when there is a *true* emergency. If there is something on fire or someone is hurt, then it may be necessary to call emergency services.

For Landlords

- Never put up with a rude tenant calling outside of business hours to report a nonemergency. Tenants need to understand that you are not on call for them.
- Don't feel as if you have to remodel an apartment or house to satisfy the tenant's needs. Renters are great at spending other people's money.
- Don't ever lie for a tenant so you can get your rent. The housing authority has many more people that

need a place to live. If you help the agency, they will help you by sending you the best tenants they have.

Bonnie was a single mother raising two boys on her own. The older had dropped out of school in ninth grade; the younger was still in middle school and seemed to be taking his education seriously. Both boys had different fathers and distinctly different personalities. Bonnie hadn't been married to either of the fathers. I thought she was older than I was when I first met her. Later I would find out she was younger.

Bonnie was an already existing tenant in a single-family house that I had purchased. She had a Section 8 voucher, which I really liked because I knew I wouldn't have to chase the rent money each month. Instead, her rent would be deposited into my bank account electronically. She claimed she was diagnosed with "the bi-polars," and was quick to point out that she could no longer work and was receiving disability benefits.

I could tell that Bonnie had been quite attractive earlier in life. She had a pretty face and a nice complexion. It was obvious that she had a nice figure at one time, but years of lying on the couch and eating poorly had taken their toll. You could see the depression in her otherwise beautiful eyes. On more than one occasion she shared her belief in God. She told me that she didn't have much, but the Lord would provide.

The people that sold me the property told me that Bonnie had an ex-husband that would show up from time to time, when he wasn't in jail. She was never married though. This father of the younger boy had recently been released from prison. He had done time for operating his own sales department out of the back of a major department store where he worked. He was selling store merchandise off the department store's loading dock after hours, all of it captured on video.

I found out from another tenant that he had come back to the neighborhood to live in the house with Bonnie and her two sons. Although he and Bonnie had never married, he referred to her as his wife when he needed a place to stay. That irritated me because I had grown fond of Bonnie and her boys and felt like they were so vulnerable.

He was a muscular man with prison tats and an attitude to match. He always had a mean look on his face—even when he smiled his face looked mean. He wore white wifebeater T-shirts and baggy jeans that hung so low you could see his underwear. I have always had a problem with people showing their underwear. That doesn't make me old; it makes me respectful. I've always instantly judged anyone who wears their pants like that. I have never felt that was an appropriate wardrobe for a man, let alone one in his forties. I didn't like this guy, and I knew there were going to be problems.

In our first meeting, when I was there to do maintenance, he eliminated any thought I might have had about his successful rehabilitation. Before even introducing himself, the convict told me he wanted some new carpeting, new kitchen linoleum, and possibly a new air conditioner. He wasn't on the lease. He wasn't paying anyone anything. I remember being struck by his boldness and having to fight back my own attitude. I wanted to tell him, *Go fuck yourself and get off my property*. But I didn't.

Instead, I stuck my hand out, offered to shake his, and introduced myself. He told me his name and said that he was there so he could be with his wife and kids. Moreover, he didn't want the housing authority to know his whereabouts because Bonnie would lose her voucher. He was correct. The contract with the person holding the voucher is very clear. So too is the law. In my region, anyone that stays over ten days is considered a tenant and not a guest. If you want this "new tenant" to leave, he or she has to be evicted through the court system. If they stay past ten days, they have all the rights that paying tenants have—which is total bullshit.

I told him that if he wanted to live there, he needed to be on the lease. I explained the law and the rules for housing, that I wasn't going to jeopardize my monthly check to accommodate him and help them with the scam. I also said that I would need to talk to Bonnie about it and then report the findings to housing, so that I would stay in compliance. I wasn't going to play the game or even act like I was playing games for anyone. He wasn't educated, but he wasn't dumb either. He understood what I was saying. He didn't like my answer but stayed cool.

I went about my business in the garage behind Bonnie's house and loaded up some supplies that I needed for a project at another home. (I owned four other houses in this area.) As I was getting ready to leave, he approached me again. He said he wasn't staying for long, and if I could just let him rest for a few weeks with his wife and kids, he would be on his way. For a brief moment I saw a human being in his eyes and I wanted to help him. I didn't agree to anything with him verbally. I just nodded and got in my old pickup truck. I started the engine, rolled down the window, and waved goodbye. Then he said, "What are we gonna do about this nappy ass carpet and kitchen flo—?"

The compassion that I was feeling seconds before quickly subsided and the angst returned. I didn't have the balls to say what I was thinking. I wanted to say *How about clean it, convict? That would be a great start!*

I shut the engine off and stayed in the truck. I explained that I had some carpeting that I was going to install in another unit but could possibly use at this house and that I was waiting on a quote from an installer. That's when Thug Daddy told me that he used to be a carpet laying professional, before he "went away."

I said, "Really? So you know how to repair or replace the tack strip, make the proper cuts, stretch it, heat it if necessary, then tack it back down?"

"For sure, all that. I can get it done today if you want me to."

My mind was racing in confusion. I knew that he didn't know shit about what he was doing because there is an actual skill involved in carpet laying. Plus, I knew I was being a pussy and trying to reason with someone who had no business being there in the first place. I feared this guy: he was a beast. The rational part of my brain wanted to tell him he needed either to leave the property or to go through the formal process of becoming a tenant; the emotional part wanted to help them. How new carpeting and flooring was going to do that, I hadn't thought through yet. Like so many times before and after, I made the wrong decision.

The carpet that I had was brand new and was intended for another unit that genuinely needed it.

Bonnie's carpeting and kitchen floor coverings were showing some wear but they were far from needing replacement. Nevertheless, I caved. Somewhere between the prison tats, the muscles, and the *I-will-kill-you* expression, I agreed. I dropped the carpeting off the next day and asked if he needed anything else. I was referring, of course, to the tools one would need to properly install carpeting.

He said, "I'm good."

Well, he wasn't at all good.

When I returned a couple of days later, I was in shock. Not only did Thugly not have a clue what he was doing, but he cut through the vinyl floor entryway near the front door, as well as the kitchen floor. He did damage to those areas while trying to make the cuts needed on the piece of carpet he was working on. Rather than take measurements and cut the carpeting with a carpet knife, he apparently eyeballed it and made cuts with something other than a carpet knife.

None of it was tacked down because he didn't have the necessary tools. It was crooked, and a giant piece by the front door in the living room was missing. It was a total fucking disaster. I could feel the heat in my neck and face. I was so pissed off. Wanting to scream at the top of my lungs but knowing I couldn't lose it, I suppressed the rage.

"Are you done with this?" I asked.

"Yep. It ain't perfect, dude, but it looks fine."

Just imagine ripping your carpeting up in your living room, cutting off the edges, leaving them frayed, then laying the carpet back down. I didn't say anything at all and turned around to leave. He knew I was pissed, and I knew that I needed to get out of there because I was already thousands in the red that month and didn't have the funds to replace the carpet and hire an installer to do it correctly. Once again I was overwhelmed, having allowed my emotions to cloud my judgment. I left.

The next day Bonnie called.

"Mr. Max, you need to have someone fix this carpeting 'cause someone gonna trip on it. It ain't safe in here, and it looks nasty."

I could hear Thug Daddy in the background, yelling about how it was cheap-ass carpet and *that* was the problem. I could hear comments like *If he thinks he's so good, tell his ass to get over here and do dis shit. Fuck, he ain't nothing but a bitch anyway.*

I told Bonnie that I would be right over. Again, I left my job—the job that was providing me with a nice paycheck, in a nice office, full of nice people. I needed to suspend my reality and go live their nightmare in that moment. Actually, I really didn't need to do anything but shut off my phone and ignore them. But for some reason I always responded immediately, taking action. Reacting quickly to this sort of problem is what seasoned real estate investors quickly stop doing. They realize that people like this will suck your soul out, call by call, if you let them. When you reward needy people with an instant response to a problem they created, they will never stop calling. They will rob you of your peace.

Driving my old Buick down the road, wasting more time away from my job, I could feel the heat rise in my neck. This time Thug Daddy and I were going to have to come to an agreement about the arrangements—or he was going to leave in a squad car. I was also hoping that I wasn't going to get taken away in a body bag. With the air-conditioning cranked, I focused on deep breathing exercises while listening to Christian radio.

I arrived, parked my car, and calmly walked up to the front porch. When they let me in, there was Thugly pacing back and forth like a Doberman Pinscher ready to pounce. His face was contorted with rage; and though scared, I was ready to stand my ground. After all, this was *my* property, not his or Bonnie's. They were tenants, not family.

I calmly said, "Bonnie, I don't have the money to replace this carpeting right now. I won't have it until next month. I didn't create this mess either. So I won't be paying to have it fixed."

That was lift off for Thug Daddy. He raced over to where I was standing—veins popping out his neck, muscles bulging, his face in mine with barely a couple inches between. I could smell his foul breath as he screamed in my face.

"You fuckin', slumlord, mother fucker. You better fix this fucking floor or you gonna have to pay with yo' ass. I don't like how you treat my wife and kids. They don't have to live in a shithole like this. You feel me, you piece of shit?"

That is when I blew. I was ready with every ounce of my body to defend myself. He was way stronger than I physically, but my rage had propelled me to a new level, piercing through my body. It was that feeling of having had enough. That point of no return. I knew that if he touched me, I was not going to lose this time. Then I leaned in a bit closer.

"You, get the fuck off my property now."

His eyes were full of rage, like the real demon he was. My eyes, I am certain, mirrored that rage. This was the first time I had pushed back, at the highest level I could muster.

"I am going to go to housing and tell them everything, you fucking thug. Your so-called wife and kids will be homeless again—because of *you* and *your* actions—not because of me. Do you understand that?"

I turned and left, then spun gravel with the Buick as I exited down the driveway to return to work. Radio back on, blaring some Christian song, I let the heat in my veins slowly dissipate. I was certainly not acting like a Christian. Instead, I was consumed with hatred.

Miraculously, the next day Bonnie called to say that Thug Daddy had moved out. They had had a big fight. She called the police—Thug Daddy was no longer allowed at the house.

I don't know what happened to him. My hope is that he got his shit together and now has a good life. He and hundreds of thousands like him have never grown up enough to make adult decisions. His boys don't have a father figure because he was more worried about his penis and partying than the people he claimed to love, his family.

Bonnie and her two boys were afraid of Thug Daddy, and I could understand why. I was scared of him too. A big, muscular, scary, mean, angry dude. I think they were relieved when they knew he couldn't come back for a while, but their poker faces wouldn't dare show it. I was relieved, too, because I didn't want to have to deal with him ever again.

The older of Bonnie's sons was a high school dropout and an aspiring musician. He couldn't play an instrument or write anything, but he could rap, and I thought he was really good. He set up a makeshift studio in part of the home and was determined to make music. His visions of the lifestyle a successful rap career could provide were stronger than his education or work ethic. He was already masquerading as a successful rapper. He understood the power of positive thinking, even if he couldn't spell the word *positive*. I didn't think he was a true artist because he didn't put in the work. He was more of a parrot. He could rap other people's work but didn't have any of his own material. Plus, he could barely read and write. Rapper Eminem could read and write, and he spent hundreds of hours on the craft of writing. This young man did not.

What he lacked on the business side of music he made up for in having sex with young, underage girls. About the time that Thug Daddy hit the road, I found out that Bonnie's older son was expecting. Specifically, after impregnating two girls, he was proudly expecting two babies, due just weeks apart. *And* he was already dating the third. No job. No education. No condoms. And no real plan either, other than to cut an album and ride off in a limo. Thanks Thug Daddy for providing the guidance these boys so desperately needed. Or maybe it was Thug Daddy's daddy that we need to thank. Or perhaps generations of irresponsible men who have failed to provide guidance to the young men in their lives.

The younger boy had a permanent pissed-off look, like his father. He was mad at the world, and I could tell. I always tried to be nice to him, thinking that a little positive influence couldn't hurt. I talked with my wife about mentoring him, if he would let me, because I thought he could be someone. It was just talk and I never acted on it, although I wish I had. All on his own, he was trying to break the cycle of poverty and lack by doing good in school and getting excellent grades. He loved his momma too. He protected her fiercely and constantly showed her love with hugs and affection. He had his sights set on football, working out whenever he could.

Bonnie was sweet and innocent to a degree. She was definitely a lost soul that had lost her will, and at this point merely existing. The look in her eyes told me that her head wasn't where her feet were. She loved her boys and provided what she could. She was always praising God. I believe in God too, so that is how we bonded. She didn't provide much of anything to anyone, other than love for her boys.

I don't believe anyone knows what God thinks. We all have theories based on our own interpretations of the Word and religious beliefs. That being said, I think the good Lord will provide too. But my belief involves each of us doing something other than eating and staring at a screen. Bonnie had free rent, free food, free television, and a free phone. I was not making a single dollar on the rentals because of my own bad mistakes. From her unit alone, I was deeply in the red.

One night, near the end of my experience with Bonnie, the phone rang at 1:30 in the morning.

"My carbon *bon*oxide detector be beepin'," said Bonnie.

I asked her when it had started.

"It has been doing it for a while, but it doesn't do it all the time."

I asked her if the battery might be out.

"I ain't checked that."

I wish I could say that I was nice and let it go, but I wasn't.

"It's one thirty in the morning, Bonnie. I get up in three hours to go to work. Why are you calling me now?"

"I think I smell gas, Mr. Max. We don't want to die."

I explained to her that the beep would be continuous if there were carbon monoxide detected. She didn't get it.

"Do you hear the detector now?" I asked.

"No, it ain't beepin'. It only beeps every now and then, and then it only beeps once."

I hung up.

It *was* the battery. But rather than change the battery, Bonnie called the fire department. She woke up the whole neighborhood in the middle of the night.

The next morning she called to tell me that the fire department came and said there was no gas leak and that the battery needed changing.

No shit, Bonnie! Really?

One of the firemen told Bonnie that the window over the crawl space had cracked as they were entering, and it needed to be replaced because it was dangerous.

Bonnie didn't stop there. She told me that she had called the housing authority and was having an inspector come to look at the cracked glass—and I needed to be there. Thus I would have to leave work again and be there for an inspector to tell me what was wrong and how much time I had to get it fixed. *No, I don't think so.*

I already knew no one else went into the crawl space of this house. Bonnie certainly never did. A crawl space is a place where one has to do an army crawl with his or her belly on the dirt to get to the gas furnace, the water pipes, and the sewage pipes. It's not a pleasant environment—cobwebs, dead insects, darkness. From the dirt floor to the underside of the house floor, the space stretches about eighteen inches. Bonnie insisted that the glass needed to be replaced because "one of the panes was cracked by a fireman that tried to crawl underneath the house"— checking for a gas leak that wasn't there.

Tenants like Bonnie are a nightmare because they are virtually helpless. While they can be kind and considerate, they are actually totally dependent on others for their existence. And because the battery in the carbon monoxide detector needed to be changed, I got a call at 1:30 a.m. Then the fire department got a call and dispatched an entire squad. Then the power company became involved, dispatching trucks in the middle of the night. Then the neighbors were awakened. Then the fireman broke one of the panes of glass while accessing the crawl space. Then Bonnie called housing. Then housing sent out inspectors. Then everyone realized Bonnie simply needed a fucking nine-volt battery.

In her mind she wasn't going to pay for the battery, even though it was in her lease to do so. She wasn't paying for anything anyway because she lived completely free. She wasn't going to pay for the broken glass either, even though she was the cause of the glass being broken in the first place.

I told Bonnie I wouldn't be coming to the inspection and would call public housing to speak with her caseworker.

She said, "It needs to be replaced, or I want to move."

I said, "Promise?"

When the caseworker called me back, I could hear Bonnie on the call as well. The caseworker asked why I wasn't going to replace the glass. I stated that I hadn't broken the glass and that I wasn't going to replace it with glass anyway. Instead, I was going to use plywood so that nothing could break in the future and no animals could get in. It made sense to the caseworker, but Bonnie insisted that it needed to be glass or she was going to move.

I then told the caseworker, "I want her out as soon as possible."

She confirmed with Bonnie that that was what she wanted to do. Stunned, the caseworker agreed, and Bonnie started packing up her things.

Three nights later, around midnight, she called and left a message, saying, "The good Lord wants me to stay, and I was hoping we could work this out."

I never returned Bonnie's call. Instead, I signed papers to shoot her down the highway to the next poor sons of bitches that had to listen to her perpetual bullshit and victim stories. The emotional side of my brain felt sorry for her, briefly. *What if I was supposed to look out for people like this?* Then the rational side of my brain said, *Adios!*

I am only one guy. Little did I know that I was in for more fun and lots of red ink in the months and years ahead.

Up the Neighbors' Asses

For Tenants

- NO PETS means no pets. Don't keep a dog in your unit if they are not allowed on your lease. You are liable for all the damage the dog causes.
- Don't try to be friends with your landlord. If a friendship develops, that is fine. But you are not friends. Your landlord is a service provider.
- Mind your own business.

For Landlords

- You don't need to feel sorry for anyone. Stick to the terms in your lease. It's a business—remember that every time.
- Do not tolerate pets if you have a no pet policy. There is no room for negotiation.
- Do not accept personal calls. Keep all communication about business.

I inherited Jan's and Carol's problems when I agreed to purchase the two-bedroom house that they lived in. They were both receiving disability benefits and had a Section 8 housing voucher. Somehow they had worked it out that they would both get benefits. I wasn't making *any* money on their house, because I had paid too much to begin with. Renting to two people who hadn't worked for some time was frustrating, and I had developed a negative profile for deadbeats. They appeared much older than I but still young enough to work for a living.

Jan, the older of the two, sat and watched television in her pajamas all day, every day. Because they often stayed up and watched TV into the early morning hours, their days started well past noon. Totally dependent, getting everything free, they were beholden to a victim mentality and quick to share ailments and struggles alike with whoever would listen. They were frequent fliers of the local emergency rooms.

Jan always struck me as someone who was fairly intelligent but had at some point suffered some sort of emotional setback in her life, stopping her in her tracks. I always wanted to know more about her story. I felt like she had given up too easily and that she possessed more value than she could see in herself.

Carol, on the other hand, seemed like she wasn't all there. She clearly had some sort of developmental disability and thought she was smarter than she was. With a high degree of paranoia sprinkled in the mix, Carol was into conspiracy theories, ghosts, demons, shadow people, and other strains of the paranormal. She had an interesting look—she rocked a mullet, the sides of her head shaved, and wore sleeveless shirts. Both her and Jan were obese and out of shape.

Jan had sad eyes and a whiny, weak voice that didn't match her large-framed body. She seemed trapped in her recliner, staring at an endless loop of infomercial television, portraying a life she couldn't access.

Carol had a readily apparent school-yard-bully vibe about her. She was willing to throw down at any time, becoming loud and vulgar, instantly and without prompting. Whether she was at a funeral or in a Walmart, she wanted everyone to know that she was *bad ass*.

I didn't know the dynamic between the two of them. I had initially thought they were lesbians in a committed, loving relationship, and I was cool with that. One time, however, Carol chirped, *We ain't lesbians, just so you know*. It was a totally random thought that didn't at all match what we were discussing.

Why did I like them? I have no idea, but I did. I knew they were both bat-shit crazy and needy. Clearly, I got something out of the relationship. They treated me like I was their savior, and this gave me temporary purpose. I didn't understand at the time that I got something out of it—at least for a while. I would also learn that their level of crazy was easier to deal with than someone who is *really* crazy.

I made the mistake of getting emotionally involved again. This is one mistake that landlords everywhere make. I trained Carol and Jan to be a total pain in the ass from the beginning because I picked up the phone every time they called. I'd leave my job to go and check on things when they wanted me to. I'd even cut the grass a certain way, avoiding all of the bullshit yard decorations they had installed. I was trying hard to keep them liking me. But I was doing it wrong. I should have kept it about business from day one. Professional, considerate, firm.

It wasn't until after I knew them for about a year that I realized Carol was several years younger than I was.

One time, while I was parked in their driveway, Carol came out of the house to offer me their rent check. (The Section 8 portion was automatically deposited into my account, with a small amount remaining, which they paid me directly.) After handing me the check, she placed her hand on my forearm, which was resting on the car door.

Leaning in toward my open window, she looked into my eyes and said, "I had a dream about you last night. It was a good one. We had a really, *really* good time together in my bedroom."

I pulled my arm back and smiled.

"That's really nice, Carol. Thanks for thinking of me. I have to get back to work. See you soon."

I knew she wasn't right in the head and thought nothing of it. I had never been unfaithful to my wife either. If I were to start cheating, Carol wouldn't have made the top 100,000 list of candidates.

They had their bedroom windows blacked out with a film on the outside, then some sort of heavy double curtain with a sheer on the inside. Their goal was to block the light completely because they liked to sleep into the early afternoon. They believed all the neighbors were either drug dealers, prostitutes, or hit men. They even swore that there was a ghost that walked the neighborhood—and only the two of them could see it.

They were both nice people. Other than the flock of pet birds in the house and the double-layered privacy film over the glass on the window panes and all the fake alarm company sign stickers on the doors, windows, and in the yard—they were decent tenants. I let things slide that I shouldn't have because they were so kind to me and my family. What I didn't see was that they were master manipulators, using kind words and gestures while simultaneously reaching their hands into my wallet.

The frequency of their calls increased to the point where it was a nuisance, and I had to tell them to quit calling unless there was a real problem. They didn't like that. Even after letting them know I didn't want to be bothered anymore, they'd call at least once every forty-eight hours. Sometimes they would call to tell me what the neighbors were up to, in detail. Other times they would randomly call to check on my family to see how they were doing. They'd even call to report something as minor as a ceiling tile that looked like "it could be dipping a bit in one corner." They would tag the voicemail with *nothing major, just wanted you to know*. I should have ignored the messages, but I didn't.

They kept their place really clean, and I liked that about them. They were always cooking and baking in their tiny kitchen. They would try to send food home with me if I was working on their house or one of the others in the neighborhood. What I didn't see then was that they were lonely. They viewed our relationship as a mutual friendship.

Jan was the whinier of the two. Her voice was especially piercing when she had a problem. She could bring you down from any high in two or three sentences. When she was worried about something, her voice alone would invariably darken the best day. She was an energy zapper for sure.

One night Jan called to tell me that there was poo coming up from the laundry room drain and they couldn't flush the toilet. That isn't good. Especially on the night before Thanksgiving. Especially when it's coming up from the laundry room drain. That typically means there is blockage somewhere outside the house, possibly caused by a tree root.

I lived thirty miles away, and they didn't bother to tell me about the problem until the end of the day. They had, after all, been up for only a couple of hours. Instead of going home to be with my family and prepare for the holiday, I went over as quickly as possible, as always. I inspected the problem, and sure enough, there was raw shit coming up through the laundry room floor. None of the drains, except the sinks, worked properly, so I knew there was blockage down the line and I would have to clear it. Knowing that I couldn't get anyone out there on the Wednesday night before Thanksgiving, or on Thanksgiving, without paying two or three times the standard amount, I told them I would fix it Friday morning, that is, Black Friday.

I assumed the blockage problem was *my* problem, not theirs. I assumed all responsibility for the issue and drove to a nearby hotel to book a room for them. Once back at the house, I handed Carol and Jan the key cards and told them that we should give the sewer time to drain back down and that I didn't want them to suffer. I was hoping they would be appreciative and take me up on my offer. The sewage wasn't in any part of their home other than the drain in the floor in the laundry room, and I was able to clean up that mess for them—which I would later find out was really *their* mess and had nothing to do with me or the sewage lines.

They went to the hotel room for about fifteen minutes, then came back home. They didn't bother to check out or even tell the staff that they weren't staying so I could get my money back. They decided they preferred to be at home and simply left without telling anyone, including me. It was a nice hotel by all measures, so that wasn't the issue. It was that they were insane. They did not have anyone coming over for Thanksgiving and they were not going anywhere. I should have simply paid the enormous fee for the drain cleaning company to come out, but I was trying to save a buck.

I called them on Thanksgiving. They told me that the sewage had disappeared into the floor again but they still couldn't use the stool; instead, they were going to a nearby gas station to use the toilet. I asked if we were still on for the following morning, and they confirmed that we were.

Next morning when I arrived at the house, around 10 a.m., they didn't answer the door. Granted, it was in the middle of the night for them. I called but no answer. I knocked some more, no response. I waited a few minutes more, then left. As soon as I was down the road several miles, they called, saying they were waiting for me. I had already lost an hour out of my day.

I turned around and drove back, knocked on the door, and let them know that I was going under the house. I wriggled into the tiny crawl space, with some tools and a rented eel, in an effort to locate the sewage cleanout. Underneath the house I could hear them talking, right along with the television that was blaring.

Once I found the cleanout, I put my pipe wrench on it to loosen it up. The cleanout unscrewed easily and just when the cap was almost all the way off, it popped, and the pressurized shit went everywhere—including all over me. It turns out it wasn't a tree root or any obstruction; it was simply too much toilet paper. Gobs of toilet paper that had been compacted was now on its way to the water treatment plant a few miles away, with the remainder of the blockage on me and the dirt floor of the crawl space.

I was crouched under a house on Black Friday, cold and drenched in raw sewage. I remember the moment vividly. I had had enough at that point. I didn't want to be the problem solver for derelicts while my wife and kids were at home. I was missing out on my kids being kids because someone used too much toilet paper.

I eeled out the sewage line all the way to the main and found nothing. It was working perfectly and there were no obstructions of any kind. I crawled back out of the tight space, threw most of my clothes in the bed of the old work truck, then drove home in my underwear—never saying a word to Carol or Jan. Somewhere, someone was watching a football game and laughing with their family. Not me.

My lease stated clearly that I was not responsible for clogs. The problem with putting the responsibility on the tenant is that some of them won't fix the problem. Instead, they will compound the problem by continuing to use the clogged toilet because they are too lazy or stupid to unclog it first. In some cases people will cause damage to the unit and possibly to other units below due to their ignorance. Determining whose responsibility the clog is can be tricky. In this instance, it wasn't my responsibility at all, and I made the mistake of spending time and money on a solution: I made a couple of trips, purchased a hotel room, rented equipment, and was sprayed with compacted sewage all because of their mistake. I was going about it all wrong and didn't fully realize it until years later.

Since I owned the other houses in this private court, I knew all the neighbors. They were tenants of mine as well. I didn't know that Jan and Carol had told the other tenants that they were helping me keep an eye on things and that I wanted to know everything. They used that self-granted power as leverage over the neighbors so that they could nab a few minutes with each of them to discuss "official business" about the neighborhood. Most of the other tenants knew that Carol and Jan were completely full of bullshit.

Then one day the two of them came home with a dog. Dogs were not allowed on the lease. None of the other units were allowed to have dogs either; everyone knew and understood this. After they got the dog, they told the neighbors that *Max told us we could have a dog so the dog could keep watch*. Naturally I had calls from other tenants that wanted to know why they weren't allowed to have a dog. I explained to them that Jan and Carol did not have permission to keep a dog.

The two of them were hiding the dog from me, thinking I didn't know. I remember knocking on the door to collect the rent and hearing it bark. They took a while to come to the door; Carol had taken the dog into a back bedroom and tried to keep it quiet while Jan spoke to me through a crack in the door. Jan was nervous as hell and told me they were sick and couldn't talk much. That's when I told her I knew they had a dog and they needed to get rid of it, immediately. Jan said, *What dog?* Then the dog barked. I laughed in Jan's face and left.

A few days went by and there was another call. "The dog is gone, but we need you to call us as soon as you get this message."

This time there was a new problem requiring immediate assistance. Constantly ill, Jan and Carol were continually going to doctors. They were very needy and always seeking attention however they could find it. They didn't have to pay for doctor visits like I did and like so many that put nothing back in the bucket. They used the emergency room for everything. If they got a cold or the flu, they went to the ER.

Jan had it in her mind that she could no longer walk and needed to be in a wheelchair 24/7. So on this call they were requesting that a wheelchair ramp be installed to the front of the house.

Most people in their late forties or early fifties don't need to put themselves in a wheelchair full time. I asked Jan if a doctor had recommended the wheelchair: one had not. It was a decision that Carol had made because it was too painful for her to walk—too painful to walk because she *didn't* walk.

Trying to help them, trying to reach somewhere deep and recognize that these two helpless women were somebody's daughters, I jumped online to purchase a wheelchair ramp. I was so conflicted inside. The emotional part of my brain was screaming: *You don't know what it's like to give up on life and not be able to move. Help her. She needs your assistance. This is your responsibility.* The rational side was calmly saying, *You're a fucking idiot if you buy this ramp for them. Kick their sorry asses to the curb and get back to your family.*

I clicked BUY on the website—$1,000 on a credit card. It cost more than two months of their rent, but I did it anyway. They were not handicapped; they were chronically out of shape. They were bloated, lazy, sad sacks that slept during daylight hours and stayed up all night worrying about stupid shit. They were stuck in a dead-end pattern with no way out.

The ramp that I purchased was aluminum and collapsible. Very nice. I installed it and they never used it, not once. They didn't like it. They wanted a new structure built on the front lawn. Wooden custom-built ramps are very expensive and have to be made to the local code if you are building it in a city limit. The code required twelve feet of ramp for every one foot of rise. The plans had to be approved by an architect, and the ramp was permanent. It would have cost me several thousand dollars.

Then once the ramp was constructed, there would need to be modifications to the home's interior, in accordance with the Americans with Disabilities Act (ADA). The front door would have to be widened; the hallway doors and kitchen, redone; the heights of the counters and cabinets, altered; and the bathroom shower, outfitted according to ADA's standards. It wasn't going to end unless I put a stop to it. This house was sixty years old, and I didn't have the money to do any of those repairs. Plus, the person requesting all of it didn't actually need it.

Again, I was stuck trying to reason with someone who had nothing. They didn't have any of their own money or resources. They didn't have a job. They didn't have to pay for anything by working for it. To them money wasn't needed because they didn't have any of their own, didn't make any of their own. They were victims of made up ailments and disabilities. What had started as an empathetic relationship was turning into resentment for the entitlement-mentality crowd. At that point I wanted to get rid of them and everyone like them.

I told them that I wasn't going to install a wheelchair ramp and that I thought they should probably look for another place if they felt strongly about it. They did and moved out.

To their credit, the place was spotless when they left. I mean that quite literally. It smelled wonderful. The thick sheets of plastic that they had stapled to the outside of the windows, however, were a major pain to fix. I wanted Carol and Jan gone and never wanted to hear from them again, so I let the damage slide. Good riddance. See you in the riding-cart section at Walmart!

You Can't Take My Front Door Off

For Tenants

- When you and another person sign a lease together, it stays that way; the landlord cannot choose who stays and who goes if there is a disagreement, since both are on the lease.
- If the lease says NO SMOKING, that is what it means.
- You cannot control your neighbors in an apartment building. If they are doing something illegal, call the police, not the landlord.

For Landlords

- Identifying severe mental illness in a tenant is important, especially if that tenant could potentially harm others in your building.
- When someone breaks the terms of the lease, you need to take action.
- Run a background check on every person that will be living on your property.

Finding tenants was always fairly effortless; finding good tenants was difficult. Sometimes I had luck with For Rent signs in the yard that displayed my phone number. Other times I had to advertise the vacancy. I would often schedule showings for multiple people and structure it like an open house. I did it this way because it was convenient for me and saved time. Too often people would make appointments and then not show up, leaving me standing there wasting more time. On other occasions they would come just to be nosy. They didn't have any intention of actually moving in; they just wanted to see the place. So an open house seemed practical.

Clown showed up in response to an ad I had placed on Craigslist for a one-bedroom unit on the second floor of an apartment building that I owned in a small town. Clown wasn't his real name of course but rather a description. And a scary clown at that.

He was over six feet tall, slender, and in generally good physical condition. He had a full head of dirty, disheveled brown hair. His thick glasses, which obviously hadn't been cleaned in sometime, made his eyes appear huge. He dressed in army fatigues and tactical boots. It looked as though he hadn't showered for a couple of days. Clown avoided direct contact with the two others that had come to see the apartment, his mannerisms awkward and jerky.

While on the front porch, about to walk inside the building, he said, "I can pay rent on the third of the month, when I get my check."

He hadn't even looked at the place yet.

"Well, we will have to work that part out," I said with a smile.

I led him and the two others up the steps to the unit, unlocked the door, and invited everyone in. Clown stayed close behind me and started telling me his whole life story the same way a six-year-old might.

I had open heart surgery.
I was in the Army.
We are living in an RV out at the campground right now with friends.
We came here from Kansas.
My wife and I are divorced, but we live together.
I roll my own cigarettes.
How much is the deposit?

There was a part of me that wanted to help this guy. He was a veteran and that meant something to me. He had a tweak that made him awkward in society and I felt for him. He seemed childlike and desperate, and part of me felt an obligation. My thoughts always went to *What if this were my son thirty years from now, and I were dead and gone? Would I want someone to help him?*

Clown had a few hundred dollars cash on him. The other lookers were either not serious or not interested. Winter had begun and I didn't want to pay for the unit's heat bill myself, so I decided to take in Clown and his ex-wife. Later I found out that not only had they been forcibly removed from their previous home but also Clown wasn't taking his medication for Schizophrenia.

My intentions were pure and mighty, but my tolerance level was extremely low. How big must my ego have been to assume that I could take care of people like this and that it wouldn't be a problem. People show you who they are. This guy was letting me know up front that he was a train wreck, but I was focused on the hundred-dollar bills in his pocket, along with not having to pay for another utility bill.

He and his wife moved in. She weighed maybe eighty pounds, and in her mid-fifties, she had the worn and tired face of someone twenty years older. Sweet and soft-spoken, she smiled in a way that hid the fact she was missing most of her teeth. Her salt and pepper hair was pulled back in a hair tie. Her belongings comprised a garbage bag full of clothing, and a purse. You could tell she was protective over Clown and had given up everything to be with him. Everything including identity. Her life was all about his—and what a miserable existence that must have been. While he couldn't help that he had extreme mental illness, he *could* take his meds—yet he was unwilling.

They had only been there a short time when one day I dropped by to check on them. I knocked and was invited in. Once inside the threshold, I was nearly bowled over by a wall of cigarette smoke.

I saw a giant model airplane, a guitar, a beautiful mountain bike, unmatching furniture, a tire, a cheap lamp, and hundreds of VCR tapes and DVDs stacked from floor to ceiling. There were boxes full of other miscellaneous items as well. Clown pointed to a bar stool and told me to have a seat. I was amazed at how quickly this place had filled up in only a few days.

"We got our stuff out of our storage shed."

I didn't say anything, but I noticed that none of the items looked like they were hers. They all appeared to be his. It was almost as if I were sitting in a teenager's bedroom with the teen and his mother. But in this case we were in a tiny living room, the teen was in his fifties, and the mother was actually his ex-wife. It felt weird and sad at the same time. The weirdness would soon overpower the sadness, however.

Within the first week he had his first run-in with another tenant who had been there for a long time. Ernie was a retired contractor who loved to drink beer all day and then pass out in his living room (his story is featured in a later chapter).

Ernie had some patio furniture on the front porch. He also stored some of his things under the staircase in the foyer of this old apartment house. Clown wanted to put some of his items on the porch and in the foyer too. Rather than ask me or Ernie, he simply started moving all of Ernie's items out of the way, piling them into a corner on the large front porch. He wasn't careful or considerate either. Instead, he was tossing things from one area to another as if the items had no value to anyone. Naturally, that caused the first showdown between him and Ernie, and the relationship was ruined from the start.

Clown always paid his rent on time. He settled in cash and would call to tell me when to come and pick it up. (I'd collect rent checks that weren't directly deposited into my account by the housing authority.) Clown hadn't qualified for a housing voucher, for reasons unknown, so he was paying his rent out of his Social Security proceeds. As I would ascend up the stairway to the second floor, I'd always smell a mixture of fried food, stale smoke, a touch of body odor, and a whiff of garbage—an odor I associated with poverty from a very young age.

Once at his front door, I'd knock. I then could hear him get up and walk a couple of steps, then start unlocking the multiple locks, which he had installed on the paper-thin door. One would have thought that he had bars of pure gold in the living room instead of old, shitty movies on VCR tapes. After passing through security, I'd be engulfed in a cloud of second-hand smoke. Clown hadn't read the lease where it clearly stated, "No smoking inside the unit." But neither did the other smokers, and it would cost more to kick them out than it would to clean and paint the units once they were gone. In addition to the No Smoking clause, he clearly hadn't taken the "No alterations to the apartment without approval" portion of the lease serious either. You cannot install alternate locks and keep the landlord out, unless you are not right in the head.

There in the living room, with some cheesy movie playing on TV, would be the rent in one-hundred-dollar bills. They were spread like the tail of a peacock on an improvised coffee table, made from a plastic storage tub. The sight of hundred-dollar bills excited me (and still does today). I used a debit card for everything and seldom carried cash, so the overlap of our worlds provided a cheap thrill—at least as it pertained to cash spread on a table in a smoke-filled room. I can't explain the allure, but I was definitely drawn to it. Many of my tenants didn't even have bank accounts.

I would usually talk to Clown about what he was up to, while his ex-wife sat over in the corner, puffing away on a cigarette he had just rolled for her. She would sit there smiling and make small talk, asking about my wife and kids, and telling me how pretty they all were.

Clown was a tightly wound dude and I could feel it. Something about him gave me the impression that at any moment he might strip naked and jump on the roof with a fishing pole, threatening to kill anyone who walked by. I felt sorry for him. Mental illness is no joke.

The apartment was filling up with various items from the "free store" down the street. At the free store, people from the community would donate items they no longer wanted. Then others in need would come and take those items for free. It was a good opportunity for people that didn't have much to get furniture, housewares, appliances, and clothing. Clown's living room and kitchen featured nonmatching end tables, cheesy 1970s art from the home décor section at Kmart, random NASCAR items, old magazines, and other weird-shit items. The free store is a nice concept unless you are a hoarder. Then it's like crack cocaine, and you can't stop yourself when someone drops off a three-legged table and an old toaster oven. His tiny apartment was crammed to the brim with items that he neither needed nor used, and it was overwhelming.

I had no idea that the one moving out all that stuff, sometime in the near future, would be me.

One of Clown's neighbors in the building was a young couple with small children. The father called me late one night.

"That crazy guy upstairs walked into our apartment and scared our babysitter," he said.

That concerned me. First of all, why was he in their apartment? Second, what were his intentions once he got in there? When I confronted Clown, he denied it. Of course he didn't do it. At least that is what he told me. It wasn't *him*. Had to be someone else.

"Who would accuse me of that? Does that guy have a problem with me?" he said angrily.

Since the couple in question had their own psychotic episodes, I chose to believe Clown. Big mistake.

Fast forward another week and Ernie, downstairs, said that he thought Clown was in his apartment too. I trusted Ernie and liked him a lot, but I knew he was beginning to lose his mind. So the next day I stopped by to see him and check if his story matched the neighbor's. When it did, I started to get freaked out. I hadn't run any background checks on Clown. I didn't have anything but cash and a lease application. According to his license, he had come from another state. He didn't have much when they moved in, but within a few weeks, his tiny apartment was full of things. What had I gotten myself into with my huge heart and pea brain?

I called Clown and told him we needed to talk. I asked him about entering other people's apartments and he admitted to "checking on" the other tenants in the building to make sure they were OK. My internal rage was about to boil over, but somehow I suppressed it. I was upset and told him that he wasn't to be in anyone's apartment, for any reason, ever! I told him that if he thought there was an intruder, he should call the police. For all other issues, he needed to call me first. Walking into other people's apartments, even if the door was unlocked, was a deal breaker for me.

After he knew that I was aware of what he was up to, the real freak show began. Again, I made a mistake based on feelings instead of common sense. This time I was putting other people at risk because of my shitty decision. The mix of stress, guilt, and anxiety about the unknown was turning me inside out.

About a week later at 2:00 a.m., he called.

"The neighbors haven't taken their trash out. They left it in the hallway, and it stinks. You need to come over and get it. Because we don't have to live this way." Click.

Knowing full well that I would lose my shit and escalate the problem even further, I didn't call him back. Instead, I waited until 8:00 a.m. the next day—a reasonable time for those of us that work and function in society to expect a call. Of course, he didn't pick up.

He was sleeping. I left him a message telling him *never* to call me in the middle of the night unless the house was burning down or someone was hurt. Anything else could wait until the morning.

Days passed until the next call. The number was Clown's, but it was his ex-wife on the phone. She asked if I had seen Clown. *No, I haven't seen him. Why?* She explained that he had gone missing for a couple of days and that his truck had been stolen. My first thought was that he had been admitted into the psych ward at the hospital and his truck would be in the damn parking lot. I was wrong.

He called later that day to tell me that he was "at an undisclosed location." Of course, he had forgotten all about caller ID, which provided both the name and number he was calling from. Clown said that rent was going to be late because his wife had left to go have sex with someone else in the parking lot while they were at a bar. He said he wasn't paying the rent until she was removed from the apartment. I never again collected rent from Clown or his ex-wife.

Removing someone from a unit because someone else in the unit wants them gone is nearly impossible for the landlord. Once the lease is signed by both parties, both parties have a right to the apartment. The way my lease read was that one of the tenants would have to *willfully* leave. Then that lease would be terminated and a new lease drafted for the tenant who remained. Instead, Clown wanted me to get his ex-wife out, which I refused to do. I told him it was not going to happen and that he had to get her to willfully release her rights to the unit.

I explained to Clown that, all problems aside, he still needed to pay the rent. Infidelities in the marriage are tragic but not a legitimate reason to skip out on rent. I would have made more progress trying to explain algebra to a squirrel. He didn't agree that rent was due. In his mind, his ex-wife's alleged infidelity was justification, and he wasn't going to pay rent until he got his way. Which he didn't.

An anonymous woman, Clown's sister I later found out, called me in the middle of the night and accused me of stealing his truck. Speaking in a slow, creepy, forced whisper-type-of-voice, she said, "We know you have his truck because he didn't pay the rent. That is really wrong of you to do that. You have no right to steal his truck, and we know you are behind it. We are going to get you."

I just hung up. I didn't even get upset. I simply pushed END on my cell phone and went back to sleep.

Clown's ex-wife called. "I am going to go and stay with my sister. Please tell Clown he can come back. I will be gone."

This was just one of twelve units that I had at the time. Who had time for this Jerry Springer bullshit? These were people in their fifties, by the way. They didn't work—they didn't have any intention of doing anything, ever—but they kept calling me. Me, the guy that was making payments on all these properties so people like Clown could have a roof over their head.

Clown moved back in. He wouldn't answer his phone. He wouldn't reply to text messages. He wouldn't answer the door. *But he was there*. You could smell the hand-rolled tobacco burning. You could hear the faint audio of some weird movie playing on the VCR. They didn't have cable or satellite, so they just played their collection of videos in power rotation. Not sure if he was ever paying attention to the movie at all.

His rent wasn't paid either. And I had given him the proper documentation for starting the eviction process.

A few nights later, one of his across-the-hall neighbors called in the middle of the night.

"It's cold in here. Our heat is not working at all. Sorry to bother you but we have no heat, and it's ten below outside."

I got out of my warm bed, dressed, and went over to the apartment building. After looking at the thermostat in their unit, it was evident that I was going to have get inside Clown's apartment. Unfortunately, the neighbor's furnace was in a utility room inside of his unit. I didn't design it that way; I purchased it that way.

I knocked on Clown's door. He didn't answer. I heard the television but no footsteps. Again I knocked. Nothing. I finally started to let myself in with my master key—even though this is against state law. I was willing to plead my case to a judge and possibly suffer the consequences in order to get the heat restored in the other unit. If I had to do this sort of thing, I would always record it on my cell phone so that I had some video. I was able to unlock the master deadbolt but had forgotten about all the other locks that Clown had installed.

Then I lost my temper. I was shouting at him through the door to open it or I was going to knock it down. Finally he let me in, and I went directly to the utility room, which had been locked prior to his breaking into it. There it was—the gas to the neighbor's furnace—*off*. So too was the circuit for the furnace in the electric panel. The only one that could have possibly done that was Clown. He had broken into the locked utility closet and shut off the neighbor's heat, knowing full well no one could get into his unit.

I turned to him with eyes bulging and blood vessels popping out of my neck. "Why did you shut this off!"

He told me that he had smelled gas and wanted to shut it off so that he could save everyone. I explained that if there were a gas leak, the carbon monoxide detector would have gone crazy, and he was never again to touch the furnace. After I lit the pilot light and restarted the furnace, I turned to him. "Get your rent paid or get out." I meant it and he got the message.

Five days later, midday Saturday, the neighbors called to report that their heat was off again. They also said that the night before Clown had pounded on their door at 3:00 a.m., stating that he was "going to chain them up in the basement and watch them die." He accused the neighbors of letting his ex-wife stay in their apartment, and he *knew* she was in there. All but one unit in the building heard this middle-of-the-night disturbance. The lot of them were freaked out. It was all my fault and I knew it.

The stress level kept mounting.

Clown's ex, in her late fifties, appeared twenty years older because of her lifestyle choices. The neighbors were a pair of youthful twenty-something guys. They wouldn't have wanted to have relations with someone old enough to be their grandma. It just wasn't happening. The scary movie playing in Clown's head— *that* was the problem.

I called the local police and prepared carefully what I was going to say, aware that those calls get recorded. On this particular call, I stated my name, then asked for assistance from an officer. "If you don't send someone with me, you will probably have to send someone to arrest me. It's not going to be good."

When I arrived, a squad car was sitting out front. After I greeted the officer we proceeded inside the building. The policeman knocked on Clown's door. Clown asked who it was and the policeman responded, informing him that he needed to open the door. Clown said it wasn't a good time and that we needed to come back. Then I said, "We are coming in one way or another, so open the door." He opened the door.

I walked the three steps to the utility room to see if he had shut off the gas and power to the neighbor's furnace. He had. This time, in front of the policeman, I told him he couldn't ever touch that. He was breaking into the utility room anyway, which is breaking and entering. He denied it and started to tell the officer that he had no idea what I was talking about and wanted to file a harassment suit and restraining order on me. The police officer had to get in his face and let him know that he was wrong and never to do it again.

He did it again. In the middle of the day.

But this time he had left. He wasn't home and the rent was still unpaid. The neighbors had called to report the same problem. I called the police to inform them that I was going over there to remove the front door of Clown's apartment and that I may need assistance.

The officer stood right there while I removed the front door, then threw it in the back of my truck. I turned on the furnace for the neighbors and left.

Clown came back a few days later to find that his whole apartment had been left wide open. Apparently, that was enough to fry his motherboard because he grabbed a few things and split. I never heard from him again.

To regain possession I had to go through a specific and lengthy process. Clown left all that stuff he had been collecting. His sweet little ex-wife stated she had no place to store it. I waited out the time allotted for eviction and then moved out all the contents of the apartment. It took an entire weekend to clear everything and then clean the place. After that came the painting to cover the nicotine stained walls.

I was out money and time again. Trying to help and think with my heart ended in total disaster. Only this time, I had put others at risk in the process. Luckily, no one was hurt—or worse.

We Found Ants and Spiders
We're Suing

For Tenants

- The lease is a legally binding contract; you don't get to rewrite the terms of the lease.
- Don't make your problems the landlord's problems.
- Purchase renter's insurance so you are covered if you damage the property.

For Landlords

- Don't ever allow tenants to change the terms of a written lease to fit their needs.
- Don't offer advice on relationships; stay out of your tenant's life.
- Require that all tenants have a rental insurance policy in effect.

Daisy sent me a text message responding to an ad I had posted for an available two-bedroom house. Though she was a beautiful girl with lovely eyes—and well along in pregnancy—her twenty-two-year-old face revealed weariness and fatigue. She worked as a nurse's assistant, providing in-home health care services, a very tough and often thankless job. She needed a place for her and her new baby to live and wanted to set up an appointment. She was very well-spoken and kind on the phone.

On the day of the appointment, Daisy pulled her car into the driveway. I was standing in the carport with lease and keys in hand, hoping I was about to meet a great tenant. While introducing myself, I noticed there was a man sitting in her car. He was studying me and following my every move. I asked Daisy if she'd like for him to join us. She turned and motioned for him to get out of the car. When he got out, I was struck by his excellent physical condition. Tyler looked like a professional athlete and was dressed in sweats and a black leather coat. He donned a thick gold chain with a medallion around his neck. I appreciated that he initiated a firm handshake, looking me in the eye.

We went in and looked around the tiny two-bedroom home. The wooden floors were polished, the appliances spotless, the bathroom sparkling clean. Plus the place smelled nice. They loved it and wanted to move in as soon as possible. I told them that first I needed to run background checks on both of them—something new I had started—and that once those cleared, I would be in touch. Daisy said that she wanted to pay three months in advance because they had just received their tax return money. I didn't like to do that because I didn't want to be stuck with bad tenants.

Tyler was her baby's daddy. This would be Daisy's first child, though Tyler had other kids spread around the country. Looking me in the eye, he confessed to being a former drug dealer (nicknamed "Ice") but now wanted to do things right. He said he was working at a local business, one I was familiar with, and was proud he had been at his new job for nine months, earning around eleven dollars per hour. He was also proud that he was clean and sober with a new baby on the way. I saw value in that as well and decided I would to help this couple with their new life.

Daisy's background check wasn't bad. She was still fairly young, and aside from a few traffic violations, she was going to be fine. She couldn't have been any sweeter while we were going through the process.

Tyler's report was as expected: arrests for drugs, assault, traffic, etc. He had a criminal history and had been in jail several times. Nevertheless, I wanted to be part of their fresh start. I liked him. I believed in him. *When was I ever going to learn?*

We met to sign the documents and transfer the keys to their new home. When she produced a wad of cash, my first thought was that Tyler was still a drug dealer. I really like cash, though, so even if it was obtained illegally, I was fixated on getting hold of it. Daisy assured me the cash was from an income tax return they had received the day before, and she could even show me the check stub. Smiling, I said, "No worries. I trust you. Enjoy your new home. Call me if there is an issue." I should have clarified what I meant by *issue*.

The crazy train started within thirty days. Daisy called me one Sunday at 5:00 a.m. to tell me that she wanted Tyler out because he was beating on her, and she wanted to evict him. She screamed in my ear about how Tyler had been fucking some whore in their bed while she was working, and she didn't have to put up with that. She continued telling me how I had *no idea what kind of a person he wa*s.

She encouraged me to come right then and hung up. I shut my phone off and ignored the whole thing. I remember staring at the bedroom ceiling, my wife asleep next to me. I felt for Daisy, imagining how horrible it must be to be eight months pregnant, stressed for money, and then come home after working all night to find the father of your unborn baby having sex with someone else in your bed.

Again, I felt like I wanted to help but didn't know how.

Tyler was a player, no question. I believed he wanted a new start but he wasn't playing straight with Daisy, and I didn't like that. But it wasn't any of my business.

Something I learned about Tyler was that he liked to keep the house clean and smelling good. One time when I was there, addressing another issue, he showed me a cabinet full of Glade products. He had sprays, plug-ins, candles, etc. and explained that he liked for the house to look and smell good because that is what his mother had taught him. That resonated with me. She might not have been able to keep him out of trouble, but she was able to teach him cleanliness. There are so many people who never learn that lesson at all.

The next communication with Tyler was on my voicemail.

"Yo, we need to do something about the bug problem in this house. Call me, bro."

Bug problem? I sprayed for bugs annually in all the homes, so I wasn't sure what he was referring to. I called him back.

"Yo, man, I found two ants in the kitchen. Daisy has seen a spider. We gotta get something done about that, man. We can't live like this, dawg."

I didn't know whether or not to laugh at him. It was the time of year where ants are *everywhere* in our region. If you only see a couple, you're in great shape. Spraying usually does the trick, but there are times when ants get in. They are ants.

"I will come by with some spray and take care of it for you," I said.

And I did. I went around the perimeter of their house with a potent insect killer that I knew would work, spraying into the crawl space, under the kitchen, and then at all the doorways. I didn't have to do this, but I did in good faith. This guy used to do a million dollars a year in drug sales, but he couldn't handle ants and spiders.

Fast forward another week. Daisy calls, coughing violently over the phone. She says her kitchen is on fire and I need to come over. I explain that I'm in another city and if the kitchen's on fire, call the fire department. She says that Tyler started the fire by accident because of the stove.

"What's wrong with the stove, Daisy?"

"It's too close to the wall."

I tell her to open the doors and windows and let the smoke out. I would be over as soon as I got back into town. Then I thought, what does *too close to the wall* even mean?

Tyler had poured a bunch of grease in a frying pan, set the burner on high, then left the kitchen to go take a shower— a shower cut short by the sound of fire alarms blasting throughout the house. Once he realized what was happening, he threw water on the frying pan. That is *exactly* the wrong thing to do with a grease fire. Luckily, he was not hurt and no one else was present. Daisy returned to a smoke-filled house right after it happened.

I wasn't about to drive three hours to inspect the burnt kitchen. Tyler sent multiple text messages and then left a couple of voicemails. "Yo, man, we need to talk—the faulty stove that is too close to the wall could have killed my family."

Had I called him back in that moment, I would have lost my shit. So I waited.

I remember thinking that I shouldn't let those calls bother me so much. In fact, it would have been better had I merely listened to the messages and digest them *before* reacting—and never return calls while angry. The calls from tenants didn't require immediate reaction. I was doing it all wrong. It was ripping me apart. It was ruining my life and I was letting it. My mother used to say *Don't borrow problems*.

The common theme emerging from all my problem tenants was that nothing was ever *their* fault. When something happened, it was always someone else that caused it. In this case, the "faulty" stove was the problem—it wasn't the moron that poured an inch of grease into a frying pan, then set the burner on high so the grease could boil, while he went to take a shower.

Unless there is an island in your kitchen where the stove is located, nearly all ranges are close to the wall. Some are built *into* the wall in fact. And they all get hot unless they are unplugged from power or gas. Plus, why would you take a shower *before* working with cooking grease? Why wouldn't you take a shower *afterward,* so you don't smell like the cooking grease? This is the type of stupid shit that ate up my time and began changing who I was.

Had Tyler owned up to it, I wouldn't have made a big deal out of it. All of us make mistakes and do stupid things. The key is to recognize it as a mistake, claim it, fix it, and move on. Tyler was adamant about the fact that it was *my* fault. I explained to him that I could replace the stove if there were a problem, but the fire damage was up to him. I called my insurance company and they sent out an adjuster. The adjuster determined that there was at least $5000 worth of damage to the kitchen, and he provided me with an estimate for repair. I had a $1000 deductible that I had to pay if I wanted to collect the proceeds to make the repair.

Tyler was beside himself. He stated that he wasn't about ready to pay that amount to improve the house and that there was no way there was $5000 worth of damage. He wanted to know when I was coming over to replace the walls and get everything back to the way it was. I knew they didn't have anything. I knew they had a baby on the way. I also knew that Tyler didn't mean to cause the damage and that it was a mistake, even if a dumb one. So I helped them.

Trying to schedule a commercial cleaning appointment with Tyler was a problem. Between sleeping until noon on his days off and slipping women into the house for sex while his baby momma was at work, he kept a tight schedule. Reluctantly, he finally let in the professional cleaning crew to do their job. They washed the walls and all the contents in the home as part of the insurance proceeds. Tyler's and Daisy's personal belongings had smoke damage, and I made sure that all their stuff was professionally cleaned, since that was also part of the insurance claim. The meager nursery they had set up for their new arrival was now clean and ready.

Tyler didn't understand that he was liable for the damage. Many times renters think that no matter what damage is done, it's the landlord's responsibility to repair it. They are *incorrect* in that assumption. In my lease, it states *who* is responsible for damage. Few people read leases and loan documents. I would have likely won a small claims case against him for burning the kitchen and refusing to pay the damages, but then I would have had to take him to court to collect the money. Because he had no money, I would have had to garnish his wages—and he was only earning eleven dollars per hour. Was it really worth it? Plus, I was still trying to recognize how hard it must be to work for an hourly wage versus making thousands of dollars in cash every day selling drugs. And now that he needed some cash, he would have to work over ninety hours just to get it.

I finally got through to him that the damage was *his* responsibility and that I would cover him and he could pay me back with some sort of payment plan. Since I had to pay a $1000 deductible anyway, I was willing to let him pay that and call it even. He said that he could do that. Then he asked, "When are we gonna get started? I ain't living like this."

After having it professionally cleaned, I had the wall fixed, then covered that area with stainless steel, in an attempt to make Tyler feel more comfortable. I never saw one penny of the $1000, let alone the rest of the money for the upgrades. And because I had filed a claim, my premiums rose.

The whole time I was dealing with Tyler and Daisy, I wondered how things were going to go after the prepaid rent ran out. They had paid for the first three months in advance. It was now halfway through the fourth month and they hadn't yet paid. Tyler texted me, saying we needed to talk about the rent. He had a new arrangement that might work out better than the current one. Since I desperately needed the rental revenue, I agreed to meet with him.

When I got there I was given a handwritten contract to read, ripped from a spiral notebook. This new, poorly written, barely legible agreement basically stated that they would pay their rent at the end of the month instead of on the first, as stated in the lease. He said that it would be easier for them if they could settle on the 28th of each month and pay their rent in arrears. He was already two weeks behind, so all he was doing was buying two more weeks—and thought I was stupid enough to agree. I explained to him that he could do that if I could collect what was due currently. But since he didn't have it anyway, it didn't matter.

They never caught up on their rent and were served notice as is customary in my state: in person, by knocking on the door. Daisy answered. I handed her the notice. She took it and said, "What's this? We have a new fucking contract?" I didn't say a word. Instead, I got back in my old Buick, wrote the time and date on my copy of the notice, and drove away. Before I could even make it home, my phone was blowing up with text messages and voicemails.

"How dare you give us this notice. We gonna sue yo' ass fo' everything you have, bitch. You making us live in a place that has burnt walls in da kitchen with a faulty stove. They be fuckin' spiders and ants in da house. We ain't gonna pay you nothin', cuz. Instead, we gonna own dis mutha fucka."

Equally brilliant messages persisted throughout that evening, overnight, and early the next morning. All captured on voicemail, which is admissible in court. I love it when they make it easy.

With court date secured, I put on a suit and got all the documents in order. I had followed the law to the letter and was once again ready to stand my ground. In my state, at the hearing, the defendant can request a trial. I wondered if both of them were going to come and make a scene in the courtroom. To my surprise, Tyler was by himself. He was wearing the same black leather jacket and gold rope around his neck, just like the first day I met him. He waived the right to a trial and ended up surrendering possession on the spot, handing the judge the house key. The judge asked if he needed to get anything else out of the house, and he said that he had everything cleared. Tyler was very respectful and well spoken. He acted like it was no big deal at all and didn't want any further problems.

I never saw Tyler again, but I did get one final text message:

I can't believe you gave my information to the insurance company. They're suing me for over $5000 for burning the kitchen. You do that to me, plus make my family homeless. You a horrible person. man.

I didn't respond.

Of course, the part about clearing everything out of the house was a lie, just like his other infidelities. I ended up spending an entire weekend removing the remaining things from the house, cleaning things up, and getting ready for the next sad story train-wreck-of-a-family to move in.

Tyler was the one that gave his phone number to the insurance adjuster who needed to assess the damage. *He* was the one that caused the damage. *He* was the one that was screwing other women. *He* was the one that was spending his paychecks on something other than rent. *He* was the one that didn't have renter's insurance. He, like so many others, was guilty of being uneducated and unaware of how things work in the world. He didn't understand that insurance companies operate as a business, and they will come after the money they lose when someone damages property. I am sure the insurance company is still trying to collect that money after all these years and that Tyler still blames me instead of himself.

Do You Take Gift Cards for Rent?

For Tenants

- Don't expect special treatment if you are renting from a friend or family member.
- When the rent is due, you need to pay it with cash, check, or direct deposit.
- Never break into your rental because you accidentally locked yourself out.

For Landlords

- If you can help it, don't rent to friends or family members.
- Don't accept anything other than money for rent.
- Charge renters a fee for letting them back into their house if they're locked out. Also charge them if they broke back into the home and caused damage.

Lawrence had a good job with the government, one that he had held for over ten years. Now in his early forties, Lawrence's life had become difficult. He had more than one child with more than one woman. One of his kids was out of high school, one was still a baby, and another in between. According to Lawrence, all the mothers were suing him for child support. He had no driver's license, loved to smoke pot, and also loved the ladies. In addition to being a sharp dresser and owning amazing shoes, he possessed a killer smile—a smile which he knew how to turn to his advantage. At about five foot ten and of average build, Lawrence had pearly white teeth and a full head of hair.

We had worked together several years earlier at a radio station. We considered each other friends and enjoyed talking at work. I always felt like Lawrence was a solid guy with a good heart, the kind of person who was happy all the time. I hadn't thought about him in years; then one day he showed up back into my life by accident.

At all my properties, I was the one who cut the grass—at least until I was able to earn enough to hire help. One time while mowing near a busy street, a car drove up beside me and the passenger motioned for me to come closer. I shut off the mower and walked over. I didn't recognize the driver, but I recognized Lawrence instantly. *How you doing, bro?* he asked. I stuck out my hand and shook his. He hadn't lost the smile, but he had lost a tooth. He looked like he was in decent shape, but the years had taken their toll.

Lawrence told me about his job with the government and that it was going well. I brought him up to speed on getting married and having two kids, but being too busy to enjoy my family. I told him that I had purchased the rental property to help fund college educations and possibly a retirement someday and that this was one of five yards I would be cutting over the weekend.

I didn't know that he had stopped because of the For Rent sign that was behind me. I thought he stopped just to say hello. He explained that he was a little down on his luck because he was being sued for back child support; consequently, he didn't have a driver's license. He also wanted to leave his expensive apartment and find a cheaper place to live, so he could save some cash. He said that he wanted to downsize, which would help him to get his life back on track financially. It all made perfect sense to me.

The truth was, however, that he had just been evicted for failing to pay rent and was now homeless (something I didn't learn until later). Had Lawrence offered the truth, I would still have helped him—I simply would have gone about it differently. Plus, he knew I would help him because he knew what kind of guy I was. I didn't realize that I was about to make another costly mistake and throw away more money and time. Because this was a friend, I completely skipped the background check to save a few bucks. Another great move.

I showed him my small one-bedroom house that was available in the private court that I owned. This was a little place, with wooden floors, that had a kitchen and living room in one area, and then a bathroom and bedroom. I had the place really clean and smelling great when he walked through to have a look.

He loved it and wanted to move in immediately. I told him I would need first month's rent and deposit. He said that wouldn't be a problem—he'd be getting paid in a few days—but was hoping he could get access before then to move his stuff in. I knew, based on my lawyer's advice, that was a really bad idea. My lawyer repeatedly told me never to let anyone move in before the move-in date, and certainly never without paying the first month and deposit—no matter what. I should have taken his advice, since I had paid dearly for it.

The little four-room house wasn't much, but Lawrence was pleased to be there. It was the perfect place for him to hide from all his responsibilities, the blinds drawn and his bong working overtime. I believed him when he said he was down on his luck and needed help. I remember how great I felt about myself when I gave him the keys. I thought, *I am really something. I am now providing shelter for friends who need help.* He was appreciative and assured me that I had made a great decision. Then added, with that killer smile, "You are my brother, man. God put us together." In that moment, I agreed, not knowing he was totally full of shit.

The first call from Lawrence came within days, when he locked himself out of the house. He had made friends with another one of my tenants in the neighborhood. Young and attractive, she loved to smoke weed just as much as he did. They became fast friends. She had two kids of her own: one was a freshman in high school and pregnant, and another was in grade school. The family lived nearby in a two-bedroom home. Lawrence had been partying at their house and didn't realize he was locked out until he returned home.

I was fast asleep and missed his middle of the night call. By this time I had learned to shut my phone off at night, so I could get some rest. Since I didn't respond to his call, Lawrence decided to get inside by breaking a living room window. The damage done, he then texted me. I called him in the morning, but he didn't answer, so over my lunch hour I drove by and saw the broken window. It had a trash bag taped over it that was being cut in the wind by remaining shards of glass. I was amazed he hadn't cut himself. Since this window was right near the door, my assumption was that he was able to reach in somehow and unlock it.

I called and left him a message, telling him that he needed to have the window repaired as soon as possible, and that he couldn't leave it that way. I told him to cover it properly with thicker plastic, or plexiglass, until he could repair it. It was very cold outside—winter time and close to the holidays. Lawrence didn't respond, but the next afternoon he called with a message saying that he needed the window replaced as soon as possible because it was cold in the house. There was frustration and urgency in his voice.

As soon as I got the message, I called him back. Rather than start the conversation off wrong, I said, "Lawrence, all you need to do is call a glass company, and they will send someone out to repair it. If you can take a picture of it and send it on your phone, or measure it for them and send them the measurements, that would be a big help for them."

He didn't like that response. "I don't own this place, man. I rent it. You need to fix the glass." This was a supposed friend of mine.

Rather than lose my patience, I explained, "I didn't break the glass, and the glass didn't break itself, so you need to fix the glass at your expense." He hung up on me.

I drove by the next day. In place of the trash bag were cardboard and duct tape, sealing the broken glass. It looked hideous, and I knew that cardboard wasn't doing much good to keep the cold out.

I sent another text asking when he would have the glass repaired. He responded, *As soon as I get some extra money.* This angered me.

I sent him another text that read, *I will fix it and add the cost of the repair, plus an hour's worth of labor, to your rent for next month.*" He didn't respond.

I fixed it later that day after work at my own expense. While replacing the glass, one of the neighbors came over and told me that Lawrence had been to their house earlier, complaining about how I didn't fix anything. Lawrence said that he had been locked out of his house and called for help, but no one answered. He said he had no other choice than to break the glass, and I had refused to help him.

The due date for rent came and went, without him paying. I couldn't get a hold of him; Lawrence had shut off his phone and was nowhere to be found. I kept showing up around lunch time and after work, trying to catch him. With each additional trip, my irritation increased. *We are brothers, God put us together* kept playing in my head. Once again, I was wasting my time chasing the rent from another tenant in a long list of takers.

Many of the people that I talk about in this book, including Lawrence, have a singular focus—themselves. They don't think about the nice things people do for them. They don't appreciate a damn thing. They don't take any kind of responsibility for their actions. They don't think about anyone but themselves. Lawrence had multiple children with multiple women. He had unpaid debts, no license, and was about to get evicted again. At what point do people like this wake up and say, "I need to get my shit together"? Why should everyone else be responsible?

When I finally did catch him on my lunch break, I got to hear his struggles immediately. There was no apology or accountability, because it was all about *him*.

He didn't say, *Man, I am so sorry*. No, instead it was "I lost my job, man. I didn't pass the drug test, and they fired me. C'mon, bro. You gotta help me, man. You know I am good for it."

He had worked for the government for over ten years in a job that would have provided him with health insurance and a really nice retirement for the rest of his life. He had never been tested before in the random drug testing that he knew was done by his employer. His love for weed finally caught up with him and cost him everything.

It occurred to me that his firing likely happened prior to his even moving in and that I was being played. He was probably unemployed when he came up to me in the street. It was probably also the reason he didn't have the money to move in. I hadn't checked his employment or his background. I trusted that million-dollar smile, my brother. I got the rent and most of the deposit around the time that he initially said I would. But it was in weird combinations of bills, like a stack of one- and five-dollar bills, then some twenties, then a fifty. It was bizarre. At this point, however, he was almost two months behind on rent, and he hadn't even said thanks for fixing the window.

I knew what I had to do. Rather than prolong it and let him turn two months into four, I needed to get his ass out. Thus I started the expensive eviction process, and the next day I served the papers in person. Lawrence was shocked.

"Bro, you all right man? I told you I would have the rent, but I am going through some rough times. Why are you messing with me, man?"

I could see the fear in his eyes. It was almost as if this were the first time I was seeing him sober. It was over my lunch hour when I served the papers; he came to the front door wrapped in a blanket. I had woken him up in the middle of the day. I told him this was standard procedure and that he needed to get caught up in rent—immediately or leave. Then I left.

A couple of hours later he sent a text telling me to come back to the house because he was going to "hook me up." When I returned after work and knocked on his door, he answered and said, "Wait a minute, bro." I could see the haze of smoke in the house and hear the television. I was standing on the front porch; he hadn't invited me in. When he came back to the door, he had a picture in his hand. He said, "You want to party with these two, bro?" He was talking about the two girls on the front of an escort service business card. "I can hook you up tonight, bro. This shit is legit. We can work off some of that back rent and you can relax."

I turned and left without saying a single word.

As it turns out, Lawrence was a pimp. Clearly, he sucked at that as much as he sucked at being a responsible adult and father. His failure to have the rent money was proof that he sucked, armed only with a plan to let these women work off some of the past due rent. That freaked me out too. Those girls were half my age and I wondered what they were getting out of the deal. I wanted to call them and tell them that if they were going to be whores, they at least needed to get a better pimp, because Lawrence was weak as shit. Then I wondered, *How many landlords actually honor deals like that?* Maybe Lawrence had done that before and gotten away with it. I knew some guys in the rental business that I wouldn't put it past. I knew how slimy they were and something like this may work great for them. But for me, it pissed me off. I was dealing with

Lawrence, the half-wit pimp, trying to chase down some rent I so desperately needed because I was underwater financially.

In my state, tenants need to be served with a written five-day notice. You can hire a process server to do this for you, or you can do it yourself. If you elect to do it yourself, you need to hand the tenant the document, which states the date and time of service, and keep one copy for yourself. Once that document is served, and the five days have passed, you can get a court date. From there, the sheriff's department or a process server delivers the summons to appear in court. The landlord has to pay for all of that, by the way. If the tenant appears in court, they are given the opportunity either to plead or to schedule a trial.

Many times deadbeats like Lawrence won't show up for the hearing in court and thereby forfeit their position in front of a judge. In that moment, they automatically lose everything. That is what I was hoping for—an easy win.

Lawrence called me the night before his court case.

"Bro, I got the rent, man."

I hesitated. I wanted to hang up, knowing full well that it was going to be a slam dunk in court the next day. Plus, I had already paid for the server and court costs, so I was already a couple hundred in.

"I have it all, man," he said.

"You're not fucking with me are you, Lawrence? You have the whole amount due, plus the late fees, plus the window, right?"

"Yeah, man. Can you come right now?"

I lived thirty miles away. My job was in the same town as this property, which is why I usually went during lunch hours or after work. On this particular day,

I had driven home and was eating dinner with my family when he called.

I knew Lawrence well enough by this time to know he didn't have the entire amount. I wanted to collect what I could before court the next day. I wanted him out of my life. I knew that even if he did give me some cash that night, he wouldn't have the whole amount the next morning in court, and I could force a judgment, which is what I wanted. I had already spent the money on the court proceedings and I wasn't getting any of that back. So why not work him over a bit? Kind of like a good swift kick to the crotch, like he deserved.

I said goodbye to my family, jumped into the old work truck, turned on the radio, and headed off to see the pimp. En route I remember thinking, *This fucker better have the money*. When I got there, the front door was wide open. I knocked on the storm door, which was fogged over with moisture from the cold. Music was playing. Lawrence came to the door, flashing the million-dollar smile. He was very happy. He leaned over to give me a man hug, which I dodged.

"Here it is, man. Everything I owe you."

Instead of hundred-dollar bills or a check, he handed me a stack of Lowe's gift cards. I didn't even know what to say. I had already wasted another evening by driving to meet with his loser ass. *Lowe's gift cards?*

He said, "I will drive up there to Lowe's with you, right now, man. You can pick out whatever you want. It's almost Christmas, man. It's your money. You can get all them tools you have been wanting and —"

"Stop. Just stop." I said. "This is ridiculous. There is no way in hell I would take these from you. One, I know they are hot as hell. Two, this isn't cash and I don't take gift cards in lieu of cash. Three, if I were dumb enough to go spend these with you by my side, on camera, we could both do time. I will see you in court in the morning." I dropped the gift cards on the ground and got back in the truck to drive the thirty miles home.

In his THC-enriched brain, Lawrence thought we were good. He had never paid a property mortgage or property taxes or property insurance or property maintenance costs. He didn't even pay child support. He didn't pay his phone bill. He wasn't my brother, and he had nothing at all to do with God.

Lawrence didn't show up for court. I never did get all the money he owed me. Furthermore, I was out the court costs and process server fees. I had to wait a certain amount of time before I could have possession of the house again. Once I was able to get back in, I found his nasty couch that he had left behind. I spent another weekend cleaning the whole place out. What I couldn't cram in the dumpster, I took to my burn pile on the property. I remember sitting on the tailgate of that old work truck, popping open a can of cheap beer from the convenience store down the street, and watching his couch burn in the night sky. *Cheers, brother*.

This experience was changing me.

The Wisdom of Perseverance

For Tenants

- Don't quit your job unless you have another job. You have to pay your rent no matter what.
- Don't knock the plumbing loose under the kitchen sink. It's best not to store anything under there.
- When someone offers to work with you, do what you say you are going to do when you say you're going to do it.

For Landlords

- Don't give anyone a grace period beyond the lease.
- When a tenant quits his or her job and has no source of income, evict the tenant.
- When someone damages your property, charge them for it. Ignorance isn't an excuse.

Tanya was an unwed mother of two. Her older daughter was about to have her own baby at the tender age of fifteen; her younger daughter was in elementary school. The three of them lived in one of my two-bedroom houses—a very small house, totaling five rooms. The tight living quarters would soon be even tighter. Tanya was excited to become a grandma at age thirty. Her younger daughter moved into her bedroom, and she purchased a crib and changing table for the other bedroom, where the fifteen-year-old slept. She was trying hard to help her daughter through all of this; Tanya had done it herself fifteen years earlier. It was if it were expected. Her older daughter looked just like her. The biggest difference in the two was that the daughter was a great student and had dreams of attending college.

Tanya worked really hard, earning around ten bucks per hour. She was employed by a home healthcare agency, which provided personal care for elderly patients in their homes. She was also working in a nursing home and proud of the fact that she had earned her CNA certification. Trading long hours for small paychecks, Tanya labored hard because she loved her girls and wanted to ensure they had what they needed. She was a fiercely protective mother and very much hands on. I recognized how hard she tried for her girls, and that meant something to me. I could relate because my mother did the same thing for my younger brother and me. Like Tanya, my mother lacked education and had escaped an abusive, toxic relationship.

I liked Tanya a lot. I would let her pay the rent a week or two late on occasion without charging her a late fee, knowing she was doing all she could. Confident I would get the rent, I didn't bug her about it. As soon as she did have it, she would text me, and I'd drive by to pick it up. There were a few times that she would pay early, if her paycheck fell on a date that allowed her to do so. I always appreciated that she kept track of the rent; I never had to chase it. She would tell me when she was going to pay and faithfully kept her word. I always felt that was the type of tenant that deserved help when they needed it. I valued honesty above all and had no reason to believe that she was going to cost me thousands.

Tanya had shared a lot with me—she was shockingly transparent at times, telling me about her sex life, her ex-life, and the people she hated. She called me one time to tell me that she wanted to buy the house from me because she found out she was going to inherit a bunch of money. She explained that she had to wire this person $1400 for a processing fee, and then she was going to get a couple million. I talked her out of that and explained the scam. Thankfully, she didn't follow through.

She was a nurturer, something she likely learned at a young age. She always tried to make everyone feel good, no matter what. She would take food to her elderly neighbors and include them for holiday meals when she had time to cook and wasn't working. She would give rides to people that didn't have transportation of their own. She'd listen to crazy neighbors like Jan and Carol go on and on with their never-ending stories, knowing full well that they were completely nuts. She even tried to help the wannabe pimp Lawrence, until she had enough of him mooching meals, cigarettes, pot, and gas money. She tried to help everyone and was no doubt amazingly caring when it came to the elderly patients she dealt with at her job. I always thought highly of her passion for others. She gave the only thing she had: her time.

Tanya had no help from the father of her two girls. He was a violent, dangerous, uneducated fuckup. He had nothing going for him other than a string of jobs. Sometimes, after a long night of drinking, he would show up in the middle of the night and pound on their door, scaring the shit out of them. She knew better than to answer. Instead, she would gather the girls, and the three of them would sit on her bed, holding each other until the pounding ceased and he drove away. He scared the neighbors, too, yelling so loudly that he'd wake everyone up. He sounded like a demon, pleading for Tanya to open the door and get her ass outside. At max volume he would call her every name in the book and tell her that she was ruining his life. On one occasion he showed up with a pistol in his hand. *If you don't come home, bitch, I am going to take care of this once and for all*—then fired a round into the gravel driveway. He was always smart enough to leave before the police arrived. They knew who he was and had been trying to catch up with him. Tanya wanted to ban him from the property and desired my help. She already had an order of protection, one that didn't seem to be doing much good.

    She didn't have a steady boyfriend. She was attractive, had an amazingly fit body and a great smile featuring a gold tooth. She was likely the target of advances all day, every day—some of which she brought on by being playful. She was a flirt for sure—but in a fun, happy way, instead of a teasing, sexual way. She liked to party when she had the chance and would have people over to the house. They would cook out, drink, smoke pot, listen to music, and watch the kids play in the yard. Even when she did go on a date, she didn't have men overnight at her house.

    Tanya was involved in a clandestine affair with a married man. She called him her "contractor with benefits." He was indeed a contractor that lived down the road from her. Working for himself, he could make his own schedule; so when her girls were in school, or at someone else's house, she and the contractor would "get some work done." When he was over, Tanya would have the blinds drawn and the house tightly sealed. He'd sneak in through the back door, executing a well-thought-out route through back yards and alleyways. I knew this because I watched him do it while I was cutting grass on the property one day. He waved at me and smiled as he was going in. I knew who he was because his wife once stopped me to ask if I had hired him to do work on one of my houses. He was clever enough to park his truck around the corner so he wouldn't get caught. She had spotted him in our neighborhood on more than one occasion and was onto him for sure. I was worried for Tanya, aware that the contractor's wife was closing in.

Tanya had been struggling at her nursing home job for some time. She told me that she didn't like her boss and that she was being treated unfairly—for example, having to work overtime without being properly compensated. This boss also made her work holidays but didn't give her holiday pay, claiming that he didn't have to. Her boss was an asshole. I remember the day she called in hysterics, saying, "I ain't got the rent. I just quit my job. I can't handle it there anymore. I had to quit." I asked her if she had anything else lined up. She didn't. She also had lost her part-time home health job because she was working too many hours at the nursing home and couldn't do both. Now she didn't have either. I knew this wasn't good, and I was worried for her, her girls, and, of course, my bank account.

She fell behind a month and a half on the rent. Her contractor boyfriend texted me, offering to do work in exchange for some of Tanya's back rent. I told him that

I didn't need any work done but would gladly accept some cash. He asked me to come to his house to collect, and I did. Who knows what he told his wife. Seeing his children when I was there made me sad. I felt like I was playing a part in the lie he was living—a lie that would ultimately hurt his family. I didn't feel sad enough, however, to hand the cash back to him, as I was always underwater financially.

One day Tanya called me and said, "You gotta come by because it's wet underneath my kitchen sink, and it smells horrible." When I arrived on my lunch break, I noticed that the plumbing underneath her kitchen sink had been knocked loose by the pots and pans that she had jammed in there. She had done this before and didn't understand that she was causing the problem by repeatedly bumping the plastic plumbing under her sink.

I took all the contents out from under the sink and set up drying fans. Then I put the plumbing back together and sealed it. To test it, we filled both sides of the sink with water and then pulled the drain to see if the water pressure would cause a leak. It was tight, and she saw that there was no leaking. I explained it all to her again; she told me she understood and would move the pots and pans elsewhere. While I was there I asked her about the rent. She said that she didn't have it and was planning on collecting unemployment for a while and taking a break.

She had worked hard her whole life, always giving so much of herself. She was doing the type of work with elderly people that no one wants to do: bathing them, feeding them, changing them, cleaning their homes. It was a really challenging way to make a living. Some of the families were mean to Tanya; so were some of the patients. I too thought a break would be wonderful for her. But I knew she wouldn't get unemployment and explained that she didn't qualify because she had quit her job. If she had been *fired,* maybe she'd have a chance; but since she *quit*, she wouldn't qualify. I recommended that she try to get her job back by meeting with her former supervisor, apologizing, and explaining that she was simply overwhelmed. She said that she couldn't go back. "I ain't never working for that motherfucker again."

Fast forward another month. Tanya was broke. She had nothing and no prospects. She was behind on rent again and the contractor boyfriend was no longer offering to help. Her plan was to apply for public aid until she could get on her feet. When she called the public aid office, they said they could help her. The requirement was that she answer phones in their office in exchange for benefits. For some reason the thought of doing this offended her. She said, "I ain't gonna answer phones in no welfare office." I tried to explain to her that it might be a really good thing that could open up other doors. That information, however, did not register. Tanya wanted cash, expecting to do nothing in return. She didn't ever consider that the office was a government agency, and she could end up with a job and full benefits. *Blah, blah, blah* . . . she ignored me.

She called a few days later. It was the kitchen floor again. She said that the floor was squishy around the kitchen sink and that she was worried that the plumbing was leaking *again*. I left the office and drove over. She was right: it was leaking. But this time it wasn't just loose; there were no pipes hooked up *at all*. The drain pipe had been hit and was completely knocked off.

Pots, pans, and other items were crammed into the cabinet. Every time Tanya used the sink, the water drained straight through, directly onto the cabinet floor. From the looks of it this had been happening for a while. It stunk like rotten food and mildew. The sour smell grew stronger as I emptied the cabinet's contents onto the kitchen floor. The bottom of the cabinet was so saturated with water, it sagged. Water had permeated underneath the linoleum and worked its way to the bathroom, on the other side of the wall. The floor was completely ruined, and I knew the subfloor underneath was soaked too. It would all have to come out, costing thousands to repair.

On my hands and knees, in front of her kitchen sink, my compassion for Tanya had reached its end. I told her that I wouldn't fix it and that she was going to have to fix it herself. Then I asked for the rent money, which, of course, she didn't have. I told her that she needed to get it somehow, some way, or face eviction. Her face contorted into a look of betrayal, maybe even somewhat shock. I knew that she had viewed me as a brother or father figure in some way. I was one of the few in her life that she could count on. But this time it was different and we both knew it. I was tired of her feeling sorry for herself and not doing anything about the problem *she* had created. She was likely tired of working like a dog for no money and no respect. I didn't want to lose my temper with her because I knew how fragile she was. But it was time for her to move on.

To her credit, she did leave. I ended up missing out on three months' rent and had to rip the floor out in the kitchen all the way down to the joists. Most people understand that you can't hit the PVC plumbing under the kitchen sink. Most people don't store pots and pans under their sink either. In most homes cleaning supplies are under the sink, along with things like garbage bags and sponges. Pots and pans are typically stored in another lower cabinet, near the stove. No one had ever explained that to Tanya in a way that she understood. Although it cost several thousand dollars to repair the damage she caused, I was more worried about her and her two girls than the money. I said a few prayers for them, as it was all I could do at the time. I wondered, Would she go back to that abusive drunk? Would they be homeless? Would the fifteen-year-old girl go back to school? What about the baby?

I was emotionally involved again, caring for them as human beings. I always wanted to help Tanya and would have been willing to go the extra miles for her and her two girls had she *tried* instead of simply given up. But something snapped and she stopped. She had worked herself past her limit and could do it no longer. In a weird way I understood. I wanted to give up too. I wanted to stop answering the phone, to turn the rental houses back to the bank, to go home to my family. I wanted people to think about someone other than themselves.

I never saw Tanya again. I really hope that she and her girls are OK—and that she isn't a great-grandmother by her forty-fifth birthday.

Sorry, Ms. Jackson, I Ain't No Fool

For Tenants

- Don't assume you are smarter than anyone because you have more education.
- Don't invent a problem that doesn't exist so you can skip paying rent.
- Don't ever write a bad check. If you know you don't have the money in your account, don't write the check.

For Landlords

- Don't assume someone will make a good tenant just because they are highly educated.
- Don't assume someone that makes a lot of money will pay their rent.
- Don't let someone skip paying rent because of an issue with the rental that doesn't exist.

Ms. Jackson responded to an ad for a vacancy I had posted online. It was for a one-bedroom home with a carport and shed. The first time we communicated, on the phone, I was struck by how well-spoken she was. *Maybe she's from an agency, trying to place one of her clients*, I thought, *or a real estate professional*. She sounded very polished. It was a treat to talk with someone who could communicate so effectively, and I was curious to meet with her.

I remember seeing her for the first time. The talk track in my head went something like, *This house is a shit hole. A lady like this will never want to rent this house. I am wasting another lunch hour.*

The home was old but clean. It was everything anyone would need, but it didn't at all match this diva's vibe. She had some serious cash—or so it appeared. Well-dressed, expensive shoes, late-model European sports car. She presented herself extremely well, exuding confidence and power. A large framed woman, Ms. Jackson had beautiful eyes with incredible lashes, attractive long hair, great skin, really nice nails, and expensive-looking jewelry. She was a classy, polished, professional fifty-year-old woman. I was impressed.

I showed her the little home. She examined each of the four rooms, asking few questions and refraining her emotions. "How much is the rent again?" I told her. "The deposit?" I told her that too. She said that she thought it would work for her, temporarily, and we started discussing the terms. I asked some qualifying questions about her main source of income. She had a job with the government as a high-ranking official in her office, which I later verified through the background check. She had also informed me that she had earned two master's degrees and was working on a PhD. Divorced, kids grown, no pets. *Perfect tenant! How did I get so lucky?*

From the moment I met her, Ms. Jackson used big vocabulary words and spoke in a way that I found humorous at times. In fact, I had to think of something bad or serious to keep from laughing in her face. She truly believed she was a higher life form, and I was buying it. Throughout our interactions, once she signed the lease, it was as if she were gracing me with her presence. I was still confused as to why a high-ranking official, who had so much education, was renting a shitty little one-bedroom home in one of the rougher parts of town. *Why is she driving a car that's worth more than the house she's renting?* I wondered.

The truth surfaced when I next met her to give her the keys, so she could move in her things. I thought she had sent someone else to collect the keys at first. But it was her. The eyelashes were gone. So was the wig. The sweat pants weren't flattering either. It was kind of like peering behind the curtain to see that the wizard was really just a goofy, fat, old man.

I bought her story of why she couldn't pay her deposit up front. She was one of those pain-in-the-ass tenants who wanted me to "work with her" on her deposit. That is *always* a red flag, but I ignored it. I was caught up in the first act of the play, buying the "educated professional" vibe. I genuinely thought she was brilliant and that we had established an intellectual bond. Little did I know she was playing me for the naive, overextended, completely stressed out, average-IQed landlord that I was.

She did pay rent the *first* month. Like an idiot, I had given her the keys without requiring the deposit—a deposit she never paid. Nor did she ever pay rent following the first month. When I made attempts to contact her about it, she wouldn't answer. Instead, she'd send half-baked text messages like *tomorrow*. She made no sense. Other times, she would text reasons why she couldn't answer her phone: she was in a class or in a meeting at work or at a press conference. She was avoiding me—and kept avoiding me until I got tired of it and left her a phone message: "Please pay your rent or get out of my house. I have a family of my own and a full-time job. You are no busier than I am. Call me immediately, and tell me when I can collect your past due rent."

I heard back nothing. Must have touched a nerve. Apparently, people who are presented with facts about their obligation get offended. Especially when they are used to being catered to based on a fake persona they've work so hard to project.

A few days passed and she called. I couldn't pick up, so she left a message: "I would be happy to pay your rent if this home weren't contaminated with mold. I have contracted an infection in response to the uninhabitable conditions here in this house. I haven't been able to talk and have required medical attention. I've established contact with one of my associates at the EPA, and we will be investigating this matter further." She coughed into the phone before ending the message.

Ms. Jackson was trying to intimidate me. What she didn't realize is that she was doing just the opposite. In that moment, I made the determination to kick her flashy ass to the curb. When I called her back a few hours later, she picked up and said, "Yes?" not *Hello*, or any kind of greeting, just *Yes?* like *Why are you bothering me?*

I said, "Pay your rent and quit playing games." She hung up.

Then she sent a text message, stating that she wouldn't be paying rent until "the chronic medical issue was mitigated." Her text continued: *You will need to provide temporary housing while this home is treated for contamination.*

I texted back: *Pay your rent or get out of my house. I am not going to play your ridiculous game.*

Ms. Jackson made really good money. I knew because I verified her job. Her credit wasn't that great, though I didn't find out why. Was it student loan debt? divorce? medical bills? I didn't know. But she made no mention of anything being wrong when she rented the house. Clearly, she was hiding something, and that something was preventing me from getting my rent.

The next day I went to investigate. I sent her a text, asking for permission to enter the residence and inspect. Mold needs a source of food (that is, moisture) to survive. If you eliminate the moisture, you kill the mold. I looked under the kitchen sink, then in the bathroom, then under the house in the crawl space. The roof was new; the attic had no leaks, no spots on the ceilings or walls. I found nothing but cobwebs and dry dirt underneath the house. When I reported my findings to Ms. Jackson, she told me that I was wrong. I informed her that I was trained in mold remediation and that I didn't see evidence of any mold anywhere in the house. I was telling the truth. I worked for a contractor and had been to mold remediation training. I knew she was trying to con her way out of paying rent, and I wasn't going to let her.

I purchased a mold testing kit from the hardware store. They are simple to use and reasonably accurate if you follow the instructions. They are a good indicator if you have an issue that needs attention. The result of the test revealed normal levels of mold in the air. I showed her. But that was still not good enough for Ms. Jackson, and she was not going to pay her rent until the problem was resolved.

This time she wanted a mold remediation contractor. My problem with those types of contractors is that at times they will find mold so that they can sell a solution. I knew that because I was in the construction business already. Plus, the simple fact remains that mold is everywhere. You can find mold in brand new homes if you know what you are looking for. There are mold spores in the air everywhere in our region of the country. Someone with a dual master's degree, working on a PhD, should know that. But common sense and higher education are not the same thing.

I told Ms. Jackson that *she* could pay for the assessment—and if unsafe levels of mold were detected and the source determined, I would pay to have the issue resolved. And no matter what, I said, she still owed the rent. Still not good enough. She was insistent that there was a mold issue, and she held firm that she didn't need to pay rent until a solution was presented. I knew the law and I knew she was wrong. In fact, if there really were mold and it were visible, all she had to do was pay her rent; then take photos documenting the mold, hire the mold remediation contractor, get a positive test result, and send me a certified letter granting me ten days to fix the issue. Had she done it that way, she would have been right and probably would have won her case in court and recouped her costs. But you can't skip the rent, ever. She was doing it completely wrong. Plus, there wasn't a damn mold issue to begin with. Lawyer up, girl!

I told her that I would be starting the eviction process immediately. She had no response.

Before I could get ahold of her, she dropped off a check at one of the neighbors, telling them to call me. Ms. Jackson suddenly had to leave town, supposedly, but wanted me to have the rent. That check wasn't going to stop me from evicting her because she was more than one month behind. I planned to cash the check *and* proceed with the eviction. I was done playing.

I deposited the check in the ATM and forgot about it, that is, until I found out it was bad. The written out amount differed from the numeric figure. I didn't notice it at the time because I didn't even look at the check. Later I learned that the legal amount is the written out portion, not the numbers in the box. I have a feeling she knew what she was doing.

The other problem with the check—it bounced. Then it hit my checking account and caused me to bounce other checks in my rental business checking account. I was running that account pretty tight in those days and needed every dollar to make the wheels turn. The bouncing of her check was just enough to trigger the two that I had written right after to bounce. My bank covered my checks, but I had to pay overdraft fees. I was furious.

I rose early and drove to Ms. Jackson's home before she left for work, her five-day notice in hand. She came to the door in her bathrobe, no wig, with what looked like a net over her head. I handed her the document, but she wouldn't take it. I asked her a second time to take the document. She wouldn't touch it. She wouldn't answer me. Her face was expressionless. She stared right into my eyes in defiance, refusing to extend out her hand. I dropped the document in her doorway, stated that she had been served, and got back into my car, noting time and date.

I knew she was going to dig in her heels and fight this all the way. Clearly, she had no intention of paying anything. She was trying to make it as hard for me as she could. I knew she would show up in court ready to talk about mold. I knew she would have documents and studies and even some recommendations from her elite group of educated friends. The only thing she was forgetting, the one thing she would need to present to the judge, were her rent receipts—and those she didn't have.

Our day in court arrived. Right before the scheduled start time, she emerged through the double doors at the back of the court. With files under her arms, a fake fur coat, and a fresh wig, she was dressed to impress and ready to get the party started. Ms. Jackson would be representing herself.

All rise.

The judge did a wonderful job of setting the stage. He said something to the effect of

> if you're here because you haven't paid your rent, I will give you the opportunity to pay your rent to your landlord today. If you are going to tell me there is a problem with your place or there are repairs that need to be made or any other excuse why you haven't paid your rent, you are going to lose today. Again, if you haven't paid your rent, I will give you the opportunity to make it right with your landlord, right now.

I went into the hall where we were instructed to go. She didn't come out. She was determined to take her case all the way.

The judge allowed five minutes. I then walked back into the courtroom, unbuttoned my sport coat, and had a seat. Ms. Jackson believed she was smarter than anyone in the room, including the judge. She approached the bench like she was royalty.

"Ms. Jackson, have you paid your rent?" the judge asked.

"No, your honor. There is a mold issue that—"

Before she could finish her sentence, the judge looked at me and said, "When would you like her out?" That was the most satisfying moment I had experienced in a very long time. Finally, someone was forced to respond to reason. As her fake eyelashes fluttered, as she stood with me at the bench, I chose to show the court I had some compassion. I gave her ten days. She had lived there free for a couple of months, so what was ten days? She was ordered to vacate on the spot.

The judge stated, "Your landlord wants to be paid rent. If you haven't paid rent, then you need to get out. You have ten days to vacate." With that, he stamped something on the document and signed it.

She glared at me. She was embarrassed by the whole thing, having fully anticipated going in there and putting on a show worthy of *Law and Order*. Instead, her ego was quickly deflated like a popped balloon. I briefly felt sorry for her as she was leaving the courtroom. She was blinded by her own hubris, and it had finally caught up. In ten days she would be homeless unless she was able to cough up a deposit and first month's rent for some other sucker in town.

There was no mold. Even though I won in court, I would have had to take her back in order to collect and garnish her wages. It wasn't worth it. Typically, when someone can't pay you rent, they aren't going to make court ordered payments either. Sometimes it's better to cut your losses and move on.

It's too easy to assume someone is poor based on the way they present themselves; it's also easy to assume someone is loaded by the way they present themselves. Both assumptions are pointless.

Walking from Helter-Shelter

For Tenants

- Don't lie on your application—list all tenants.
- Don't let your kids tear up the house. You are responsible for your kids' actions.
- Don't lie about your income to get in the door.

For Landlords

- If a tenant is lying on the application deny them access.
- If the tenant does not have verifiable income plus the first month's rent and security deposit, deny them.
- If you know your tenant is putting a child in danger, inform your tenant that you are going to call protective services, and then do it. Protect the children always.

It was unusually hot and humid the day Brenda came walking up the gravel drive at one of my rental houses, pushing a stroller that held two little boys. One was preschool age and the other around a year old. She appeared somewhere in her early twenties, was grossly overweight, out of shape, and sweating. Her hair pulled back tight, her teeth yellowed. On her face was the look of dread and shame. The kind of look that makes you want to avert your eyes. She was desperate and I knew it. Desperate people repel instead of attract. She made me uneasy. The only reason I showed her the house was because of those two boys. Children don't choose their parents. Both kids wore diapers, nothing else, and they were dirty. The youngest looked as though he were going to pass out from the heat. I felt horrible for all three of them. It was as if God were tapping me on the shoulder again, wanting me to help and give them a home. Brenda told me that she had been living in the shelter and needed a place. She had nothing.

My mind always races to what someone like this experienced as a child themselves. Did she have good parents? Did she spend time with her family in a shelter when she was a child? Was this the only way of life she had known? Are her parents living and involved in her life? What brought her to this point of desperation—a series of missteps? drugs? a young man?

The shelter she was living in was downtown, five miles away. She liked my house primarily because it was close to the city bus line. Not having a car, she had to take the bus to meet me, then walk along a very busy four-lane roadway, pushing the stroller with the two boys. She had called me about an ad that I had placed online, and we arranged to meet during my lunch hour. She was about twenty minutes late, but after I saw what she had to go through to get there, I didn't mind. The house was old, but it was clean and everything worked inside. It was the house that Mariah, from the first chapter, had lived in. I had just repaired all of Mariah's damage from months earlier and had the house looking and smelling great.

Brenda walked through the place and said that it would be perfect. I asked her how she was going to pay her rent, and she said that she had just received a voucher from the housing authority and that another agency was going to give her the money for the deposit. I told her that I would have to verify funds before I'd sign a lease and give her the keys. She understood. Placing myself in her shoes on this sweltering day with two little kids in a stroller and no options, I felt an overwhelming urge to help her. She needed assistance.

Once again I thought about my own mother and how she must have felt when she needed a place for my brother and me, and had nothing. My mistake was comparing Brenda to my mom, but Brenda wasn't the same type of woman as my mother. Not even close. She wasn't working; she hadn't worked at all. Plus, she had a third child on the way that she wasn't telling me about. No education, no identifiable skills, and certainly no plans. She was simply existing. Still I felt bad for her and wanted to help, to get the three of them into a house and off the streets.

I had driven my old Buick to the lunch-hour appointment. After I showed and locked the house, we headed outside to wrap things up. I then turned my head in horror: the older kid had climbed into my car through a window that was rolled down. I kept listening to Brenda drone on about her misfortunes as the kid was turning dashboard knobs, opening the glove compartment, grabbing contents and throwing them out the window onto the gravel drive. Brenda kept talking, oblivious to what was happening. I walked over to my car, opened the door, gently grabbed the little guy by the arms, and put him back in the yard. Then I rolled the windows up and locked the door. Brenda continued rambling as if nothing had happened. I was pissed that she was that out of it and fought the urge to end the whole thing right then. Like most responsible people, I don't like being around out-of-control kids and their unaware train-wreck parents.

Before Brenda could move in, the housing authority needed to inspect. They wanted me to put new screens on all the windows. I did so reluctantly, considering the couple hundred bucks and time it cost me. Renters are always hard on screens for some reason. Maybe it's because they can't slow down long enough to think their way through how to operate them correctly. I never understood why someone would want to take the screen out anyway. That seemed odd. I understood opening the window for some fresh air, but taking the screen out made no sense to me.

After putting in the new screens, I installed new fixtures in the bathroom, including towel bars, a toilet paper holder, and a new vanity with a mirrored door. I was genuinely excited to see this young mother and her two boys get off the streets and into a home, and I wanted it to be as nice as possible for them. I felt a sense of pride.

I had to agree to a lower monthly rental fee in order for Brenda to get in the house. The housing authority offered rental assistance, citing a social security income that Brenda was supposedly receiving. That would mean that she would have to pay me a small portion on her own out of those proceeds. I agreed to reduce the monthly rent by the amount proposed in order for her to get in the house. I would raise the rent back to the normal rate once she had more income. After the agreements were made and signed, I received the rent from the housing authority and the deposit money from the homeless assistance agency. I got a call from the director of that agency, thanking me for helping Brenda and her two boys get off the street. The director said, "I wish more landlords were kind like you." I felt like correcting her and saying, *You mean you wish more landlords were suckers like me, helping people that won't help themselves.*

On move-in day, Brenda was transported to her new home in a church's minivan, all of her belongings stuffed into black plastic garbage bags—a bag of toys, a number of bags with clothes, and a few odds and ends for the house. She dumped everything onto the living room floor. Brenda did not look happy; she looked overwhelmed. I wished her well and told her to call me if she needed anything—something I always regretted saying minutes afterward. Mainly because she needed *everything*, including the will to live, the motivation to get off the floor, and a sense of purpose that would help her rise. She was a mess.

The first complaint came just days after her moving in. She sent a text that read, *The closet door fell off.* Instantly, my mind went to the dark side. I was several years into my landlord experience by this point, and my tolerance for lying was very low. The door she was referring to rolled on rollers, in tracks at the top of the door. They don't "fall off." To get the rollers out of the tracks, they have to be lifted at an angle; I knew that much before even going over to inspect. When I arrived to have a look, my thoughts were confirmed. Not only was the door off the track completely, but it had a hole punched through it the size of a fist. Now that really pissed me off. I asked her about it, and she said, "That was there when we moved in." I knew clearly that it wasn't because the housing authority had done a thorough inspection of each room—an inspection which she was given a copy of.

To add to my frustration, the new screen that I had placed on the door, just before Brenda moved in, was already poked through and ripped. There was trash all over the living room floor; it looked like a campsite instead of a living room. Her older son had written on the walls and the wooden doors with a permanent marker. Outside in the carport, trash was collecting. The dumpster that was provided as part of the rent was some fifty feet down the lane. She didn't bother with taking her trash to the dumpster. I don't think she moved much at all, actually.

I wanted to scream in her face and tell her that she needed to take responsibility and recognize that several people had collaborated in her behalf to get her in a house and off the street. I refrained, however, and instead made several trips from the carport to the dumpster with bags of stinky, nasty, dripping trash. There was a fowl stench in the carport from a stain that had formed on the cement floor, flies buzzing all around. I sprayed the carport floor with a water hose and pushed a layer of greasy brown sludge off the cement and into the grass. The smell was overwhelming.

As I was leaving, one of the neighbors flagged me down. I stopped my car, rolled down the window, and listened in horror as he told me about Brenda's older son. He was going into homes in the neighborhood, including his. Apparently, the little boy was always running wild, and on more than one occasion had entered a neighbor's house, that is, in addition to getting into cars and rummaging around. It was clear that Brenda had no control whatsoever. I apologized and told the neighbor that I would have it stopped.

He went on to tell me how the boy's father came to get the boy from his house one afternoon. I said, "Wait, what?" He gave me the description of a large, overweight, stinky man with short black hair, living in the house with Brenda and the kids. Supposedly, this guy had been staying there the whole time, and I had no clue. Brenda was a pathetic liar, but this dirtbag was smart enough to stay out of sight. She had never mentioned this guy; I didn't know he even existed.

I turned around, went back to the house, knocked on the door, and questioned Brenda. She told me everything. She admitted that he was the father of the boys. She said that there was an existing Order of Protection on him, that he was bad news, and that if she listed him on the lease she couldn't get any assistance. That's why she lied and never told anyone about him. Brenda wanted to get away from him. He wasn't allowed at the shelter that she had come from either. He was the primary reason they had no place to live. He didn't work. He played video games all day and night. He didn't contribute anything and was abusive. He was the one that got them evicted from other places they had lived and was the chief reason they were all homeless, according to her.

I told her that he was not allowed to stay in the home under any circumstances and that I was going to tell the housing authority. She begged me not to, saying she would be homeless again if I did. She was wrong: she and her boys were on the lease, without this loser, and this was her chance. I assured her that I would help, *but* she couldn't allow him in the house. She didn't respond. Typical of abusive relationships, this guy had power over her. I was determined to run him off even though I had never seen him nor had any information on him, including his real name.

After that conversation, things got progressively worse. One day while driving by, trying to catch up with "the gamer," I saw the new storm door flapping in the wind, its screen lying in the yard. I went up, knocked on the door, and asked her about it. She said, "There was a bad storm." Again I had the urge to scream in her face, but I didn't. She was a liar. She was under the grip of a total degenerate loser. Obviously, no one was going to take responsibility. I removed the screen door entirely and took it with me. I figured if she didn't know how to take care of it, she didn't need it. Like so many I witnessed before her, she neither valued nor respected other people's property.

Fast forward several days and Brenda calls from the hospital. She had turned on me. She was shouting over the phone, saying that her preschooler had third-degree burns on his feet from the house furnace, and she was going to call housing to file a formal complaint because the house was not safe. Then she warned me: I would need to replace the furnace system and pay her for damages, and she was going to sue me for her son's condition. "Fuck off!" I said and hung up on her.

The furnace she was talking about was in the hallway. It had been there fifty years, inspected by the housing authority, and serviced by a professional heating-and-air contractor. There was no way the burns on her boy's feet were from that furnace. I was full of rage. I had spent money to get her into the home, accepted a reduced rental fee, looked past her lying to me, and accepted the damage she had done to my property, knowing she'd never pay to have any of it fixed. I was not going to be threatened with a lawsuit on top of everything else by her sorry fat ass! Enough was enough, yet again.

I called the housing authority and explained to her case worker that the furnace grate does get hot, but *not* hot enough to burn feet. A quick touch would be enough for anyone, including a five-year-old, to realize not to leave his feet there. Putting on socks would have been a straightforward solution, but Brenda didn't clothe her boys most of the time; they likely would never have had on socks or shoes.

The hospital had contacted the Department of Children and Family Services (DCFS), and an investigation yielded that the burns had nothing to do with the furnace. I never found out what the burns were from, but I know *I* didn't have anything to do with it. Brenda had to undergo an investigation and was facing losing her two boys. She was about to give birth to a third, and DCFS was all over her about her plans to care for the newborn. Good. Thank God!

I didn't hear from her for a few more weeks. The next call from Brenda was to tell me that she wanted to move out and needed me to sign papers allowing her to leave. I asked if she had a place to go, and she stated that she did. I told her that I would gladly let her out of the lease as long as I was paid through the end of the month and that she had to be completely moved out before I signed anything. I wasn't about to get stuck with Brenda still in the house *and* sign documents giving up the rent money at the same time. She hadn't paid for anything the whole time. Not one cent. Nor did she appreciate anything from anyone.

She did leave, but she left all the furniture that had been donated to her. She also left behind an entire house full of trash, dirty diapers, lots of fast food packaging and pizza boxes, and a toilet full of feces. The walls in every room were scribbled with black permanent marker. Plus, she left a car she had managed to acquire from a "buy here, pay here" lot. I had to call the dealer and tell them to come and take their car back. They showed up only to discover that the car wasn't running and also had a flat tire and broken windshield. She hadn't paid them anything either. One of the representatives had the nerve to ask me how I was going to pay for the damages. I laughed in his face. "Get that piece of shit off my property or I will drag it to the dump myself."

It took about a month to clean up and get things back in order. The time-consuming painting, repairing, replacing, cleaning, all had to be done once again. Plus, I had to find a home for all the furniture that was donated to her from people with good intentions. What a complete mess. I never heard from Brenda again. One of the neighbors said that she moved back closer to her parents in another city. I thought that move might be good for Brenda's children, but I felt sorry for Brenda's parents.

I am not a qualified mental health professional, clearly, but I have common sense. At what point do people like Brenda stop taking handouts? At what point do they recognize that others are trying to help them, and all they have to do is put in some effort? Clearly, Brenda had created a nightmare for herself. Her life was a ball of stress. But she didn't appear to be doing anything at all about it. People like her make it hard for people like me to give a shit. The only reason I cared in the first place was because of those two little boys. I wanted to help them. But Brenda kept messing it up for all of them. I was relieved she was no longer my problem. I would much rather have had that house sit empty than have to clean up after another person like her.

I wasn't done yet.

Drunken Dementia

For Tenants

- Don't paint anything without permission.
- Don't turn on the stove, then fall asleep.
- Don't remove batteries from your smoke and carbon monoxide detectors.

For Landlords

- Some tenants are not fit to live on their own. Call the tenant's family to get the person out.
- Don't let tenants destroy your property and then expect you to fix it.
- Schedule annual inspections with tenants and thoroughly go through each unit, making notes. Sometimes it's easy to assume everything is OK with a long-term tenant, when it's not.

Ernie was a retired contractor in his late sixties with three adult children and an ex-wife. He dressed in satin jackets and blue jeans. Ernie didn't own a car—not sure if he had a driver's license. He didn't have a phone in his apartment, either, and didn't believe in cell phones. He lived in my old two-story Victorian house, which was divided into five apartments. For a short time Clown, from a previous chapter, lived directly above him. I really liked Ernie; he was one of my favorite tenants. We would make each other laugh. I enjoyed spending time with him after doing maintenance or cutting the grass at the building.

Before my purchasing the building, Ernie had lived there for years, his belongings spilling out from his apartment into the foyer. He had stuffed the closet under the stairway leading to the second floor full of random items. He had more than one "God's-eye" made of yarn, hanging on the wall in the foyer. There were also random calendars, a street sign, a picture of Jesus, and a few other sundries nailed to the walls in that area. That wasn't his space to decorate, but he didn't care. He was the *un*official superintendent of the building. His apartment was on the first floor, the first apartment you saw walking up the front steps onto the porch and into the foyer. He felt this space was his, and no one had ever questioned it.

I considered Ernie a friend. He was a short man with graying strawberry-blond hair and mustache to match—always smiling, very nice, saying something funny every time I saw him. Ernie had served in Vietnam and was a frequent flier at the Veterans of Foreign Wars (VFW), a couple of blocks from his apartment. He loved to drink beer. Old Milwaukee was his favorite and he purchased it by the case. He probably drank more Old Milwaukee than anyone in town. He was well known in the local bars. He had blacked out and hit the deck more than once while seated at a bar stool. On more than a couple of occasions the ambulance had to be called. But after a brief blackout, Ernie would "come to" again and be just fine. I think everyone that knew him loved him; his fellow patrons at the bar looked out for him, and that was a good thing.

Many of his tools, which he had collected over the years, were packed and stacked in the foyer along with the decorations he had nailed to the walls. He threw drop cloth over the top of the junk piles, attempting to camouflage the mess. When I purchased the place I asked him to start thinning things out, hoping to clear that space completely.

Ernie was a collector, bordering hoarder status. His assortment of guns and knives were hanging by nails on a wall in his living room, which had ten-foot ceilings. He had things nailed from the floor to about eight feet high on three out of four walls. Mixed in with the handguns and knives were plates, old pots and pans, coffee mugs, and other random items. I felt like someone could survive in the wild with his wall-hanging collection. I always wanted to inquire what his criteria were in determining what deserved a spot on the living room wall, but never did. It was overwhelming when you walked through the front door into his apartment, but it created a vibe, each item representing a part of his soul.

The collection sprawled to other parts of the house.

Once in the kitchen, you would see his accumulation of bird nests. Those freaked me out because I knew how much disease bird nests could carry. He said he had bleached the nests before bringing them into the house. I didn't ask any more questions after that, but I should have. Did that mean he sprayed them with bleach, drenched them in bleach, or what? He had around twenty-five bird nests piled on top of the kitchen cabinets and shelves. Where did he find them all? How did he get them? Did he climb up in the tree each time? I knew he was a contractor for years and assumed that he just ran into bird nests at random job sites and decided to bring them home and start collecting them. I had never seen a bird nest collection in my life; for some reason I thought it was cool.

Ernie loved watching old war movies and westerns. He'd find them on a cable channel or play them on his old VCR. He had quite a collection of dated VCR tapes. Too bad I didn't think to pass on Clown's tapes that he had left behind. Ernie didn't smoke but his apartment had a distinct aroma of fried food, stale beer, and an ashtray. It could have been the smell of his clothes from sitting in the VFW all night.

He had a ten-foot-long albino boa constrictor living in an oversized glass aquarium, which sat in his living room. I didn't allow pets in the building, but I made an exception. One, because Ernie was harmless; two, because the snake was old and would likely die soon. In the summer time Ernie would transport the snake to the aquarium he had set up on the front porch, letting it get some fresh air. My son, who was barely a teenager at the time, often helped me cut grass at this apartment building. Ernie invited him to watch a feeding one Saturday morning on the front porch. Bite marks scarred his hands from where the snake would strike trying to snatch the rat dangling by its tail from his fingers. That day was no exception. He yelled at the snake as if it were listening and somehow knew it made a mistake. "You dumb sonovabitch, that's my fucking hand. I'll cut your fucking head off." My son and I laughed until we had tears coming out our eyes.

Ernie kept the live baby rats in another aquarium on his living room floor, having purchased them from a pet store. He covered the aquarium with an old window screen, which kept the rats from jumping out. Unfortunately, on one occasion, they escaped. Ernie found all but one.

Now, rats grow very quickly, and I was hoping that if the rat escaped his apartment, it would die in the walls of the old house and not cause a problem for anyone. A week later the woman who lived upstairs called me, screaming, "I just saw a rat scamper across my living room floor! I am calling from my couch, and I will not step on the floor until you come and get that rat out of here!"

When I arrived, she was still standing on her couch, phone in hand, watching television. She pointed to where she thought the rat was, underneath a book case. I crouched down with a flashlight and small net, and took care of the rat. That woman moved out soon after that incident. Can't say I blamed her.

I had always wondered why one of Ernie's bedroom windows was covered with plastic. One day I asked him. It was then that I discovered how he'd get into his apartment when he locked himself out. More than once, he came home drunk, realizing he had forgotten his key. Because he didn't own a phone, he couldn't call anyone. It never occurred to me that there was no longer any glass in the window. Ernie had purchased some heavy, thick black plastic and tacked it up as his temporary window until the next time he needed to break in. Then he would climb up on the central AC unit outside his bedroom window, rip the plastic open, and dive into his bed. I wondered how many nights he had slept with that plastic flapping in the wind all night, his organs working through a barrel of Old Milwaukee that he had just consumed.

There were many times that I could have kicked Ernie out. I didn't want to. He was a veteran and a hard worker for most of his life. He was nearing the end and he loved his little apartment, so I tried to work with him. There was one time in particular that I went to collect rent. He told me that he had already paid me. One thing I always did was offer a receipt. He *hadn't* paid me. This was the first time I realized that Ernie might be slipping away a bit: he argued with me and said that he had just paid me the day before. He went on to say that he couldn't find his snake. I was sitting in his living room with him. I pointed to the aquarium and told him the snake was right there.

"Not that one, the other one," he said.

"What other one?"

"The big one."

I was really freaked out. I didn't want to look around the apartment for a snake that was bigger than the one in the aquarium. I didn't know if he was serious or if he was losing his mind. I took off within seconds of his telling me that.

I contacted his son and let him know that his father hadn't paid rent. I realized it wasn't his son's problem, but I knew he would talk to his dad. His son, being the guy he was, offered to send me a rent check each month instead of my collecting it from Ernie. His son had already been taking care of some of his father's other bills and had control of his checking account. That sounded like a great plan to me, and it worked well until the day Ernie moved out. I also confirmed with him that Ernie didn't have a second snake. That was a relief because I didn't need a boa constrictor on the loose in that apartment building where other families lived.

Slipping into dementia has to be scary, not only for the victim but for the family. More proof of Ernie's mental decline manifested the day he called to accuse me of stealing from him. "Bring my guns back. I know you have them." I assured him that I didn't have his guns, and rather than make a big deal of it, I called his son. Turns out his sons had the guns. They had removed them from his home and were storing them in a safe place.

Another time when I arrived, I realized the entire front porch had been painted a different color. It was a nice paint job—but the paint didn't match the rest of the house. It was painted in an Irish Green and my first impression was *What the fuck is that?* Plus, no one had asked me if it was OK to paint the house. I questioned Ernie about it, and he said, "That's been that way for years," as if *I* had lost my mind. I couldn't help but turn my head away and laugh. It was fresh paint and it didn't match. I asked another one of the tenants about the new paint, and they said Ernie had painted it a few days earlier. I never mentioned it again. I didn't want to tell his boys either. It was just paint after all.

I found out that Ernie had changed the locks on his front door too. That is something that is *not* allowed, ever, and it wasn't like Ernie to do something like that. The local locksmith, whom Ernie drank beer with at the VFW, had changed the locks for him. Even the locksmith should have known better than to change an apartment building deadbolt without the owner's consent, but apparently he did not. I had never needed to get inside Ernie's apartment when he wasn't there, so I wasn't that worried about it, but it irritated me.

Clown's ex-wife, who lived directly above Ernie, called me one night, saying that the entire foyer and stairway leading to the second floor was filled with smoke and it smelled like burnt food. She said that smoke was bellowing out Ernie's front door, which was cracked open about six inches. When I arrived later and knocked on the door, there was no answer. I opened it a little more and peeked my head in. Ernie was curled up on the couch. I called out to him a couple of times from the doorway. He was in another world. Turning over he said angrily, "Whaddaya want?"

It was hard to breathe, and I told him that he had a fire. He asked why I thought that. I asked him if I could come in; then he followed me to his kitchen. We found tiny charred pieces of something he was trying to cook and evidence of flames on the wall behind the stove. I helped clean up the mess and air out his place. He was insistent that he didn't do it. He got upset and said, "Someone must have come in while I was napping and tried to cook something. They could have killed me." Then he asked how I got into his kitchen. He was really confused.

I checked the smoke detectors and saw that the batteries had been removed. That is something else renters should never do. In most states, smoke and carbon monoxide detectors are part of the *landlord's* responsibility. The batteries are the *tenant's* responsibility. In this case, Ernie simply removed all the batteries and then forgot to replace them, which could have cost him his life and the lives of anyone else in the building. I called his son. He apologized, then removed the stove and took it to his own storage shed. His thought was that his dad was going to burn down the building and kill people; he wanted to remove the stove temporarily while they found a place for his dad to go. He and his other siblings decided it was time to move him into an assisted living situation.

Ernie grew increasingly delusional and withdrawn. It was very sad actually because he was always a total pleasure to be around. Ultimately, his children moved him into a new place, prepared just for him, with a family member. There he would receive help with everyday tasks and live a better life. That made me happy.

His apartment had to be gutted. New everything. He had been urinating in the bathroom sink for years. I didn't know because he rarely ever reported a problem with anything. He had been shoving various items under his bathroom sink and had never noticed the loose plumbing. Everything that was going through the drain was actually going into the bottom of the vanity. Once that was soaked and had rotted, the fluids made their way into the floor and subfloor. There was no telling how long it had been that way. The entire bathroom ended up having to be ripped out. I had to strip the flooring down to the joists—that's how overpowering the smell was. Then I had to rebuild it all from the ground up. The same was true for the kitchen. It had been ignored for many, many years. That unit was out of commission for several months as I gutted and remodeled it all.

The snake was found in the dumpster behind the building by another tenant, after Ernie had moved out. The tenant told me that he nearly had a heart attack when he saw it. He was chucking his garbage in the dumpster when he noticed part of the snake's thick body sticking out of a black plastic garbage bag, which was lying near the top.

A few months later I learned that Ernie was doing much better. He was finally eating better, had better hygiene, and loved having someone around to combat the intense loneliness. He wasn't drinking as much, either, and seemed to be enjoying life.

* * *

I remember the night one of my friends got a new iPhone featuring an innovative service called Siri. A few of us were sitting on his deck having cocktails and smoking cigars. I grabbed his iPhone to try Siri for the first time and said "Siri, show me gentlemen's clubs in the area," thinking I was being cute and could get a laugh. Nothing could have prepared me for what Siri offered.

One of the choices on the list of "gentlemen's clubs" was a new one that had the same address as one of my houses. Turns out that one of my newer tenants, who was also a taxi cab driver, was running an escort service out of the two-bedroom home he was renting from me. I had no idea. He had paid the Yellow Pages for the ad and listed his home address as the place of business— his home address was one of my rental houses.

I couldn't make this up. I am not that creative. I am not talking about Lawrence, the halfwit pimp from a previous chapter either. This was an entirely different person. I sat there and stared at the new iPhone screen in disbelief. My name was now officially tied to a "gentleman's club" in a way that I didn't anticipate. The other guys sitting around the table were dying laughing. They said, "The Slumlord made Siri! Hey, let's go to your gentlemen's club and get a free lap dance."

I didn't feel anger. I knew I was done with it. I knew I was done with all of them. All of the seedy, scheming, shady losers that posed as victims. I knew it was time to put it all down and get on with life. I enjoyed the cigar, took a sip of my ice-cold bottle of beer, and thought, "Cheers to slumlord me."

Conclusion

I spent ten years with an endeavor that wasn't at all like I thought it would be. Instead of fixing up properties, I spent time trying to fix people that couldn't be fixed. I believed I could change lives with kindness. That's Hallmark stuff, not the domain of a slumlord. How wide-eyed of me to think that I could fund college for my kids and retirement for myself in the process. It was a total waste of some of the best years of my life.

The biggest change in me—the unfortunate outcome of my experience—is that I no longer care about people as much as I once did. Plain and simple, I just don't give a shit. I am less empathetic, less compassionate. The experience that I thought would be so rewarding—believing I could be a savior—turned out to be horrible, profoundly horrible. I was stressed the entire time I owned the properties.

One month, for instance, I received rent from only four out of my twelve units, all of which were being rented. It was hard for my family to make it that month since we were footing the bill for eight other households. Eight. I had to come up with fifteen thousand dollars out of the clear blue sky to meet my monthly obligations. There were also some major expenses like two water heaters, a central AC unit, and property taxes (which are among the highest in the nation). It was maddening, to say the least. Especially since I was working full time while many of these lazy freeloaders were sitting on their asses doing nothing.

The forty-year-old version of me, when my landlord adventures began, is nothing like the fifty-year-old version. I would be a much better landlord now from a business standpoint because I would keep it about business. No whiny victim stories would be accepted. For example, I am a cosigner on a lease for a New York City apartment. The company that owns that building didn't mess around. I had to submit a financial statement and prove that I made forty-five times the monthly rent. This had to be notarized. Then I had to have a spotless background check. We had to submit the first month's rent, the security deposit, and a real estate fee up front with the application. All with no guarantee we would get it all back if we were denied for any reason. It's strictly business and they don't dick around with stories from sad sack losers.

The forty-year-old version of me would have been offended by the whole process in NYC. The fifty-year-old me totally gets it. If you *put shit in, you get shit out*. That is the biggest lesson I learned. Save yourself the time and anguish up front. Amen! By the time I had learned this though, it was too late to get rid of all the low-end stuff and spend my money on better properties where I could attract better tenants. I got what I deserved because I didn't think it through; I jumped in.

Now I wouldn't even *listen* to the stories of hardship. Instead of listening to these tenants' pitch, I would cut them off mid-sentence and say, "I am sorry for all of your bad luck. Do you have the first and last month's rent and the security deposit in cash? If not, our conversation is over." Then I would move on without hesitation, displaying the detached coldness that these people likely experience frequently.

While working on this book with my editor, she point blank asked me if the struggle was so intense and the joy of life so little, did I ever think about taking my life? Yeah, absolutely. Inside I was filled with darkness. I thought about ending it all and making it look like an accident. I had a sizable life insurance policy that would have paid everything off and left a million dollars for my family. I had spent our savings and tarnished my credit. Taking myself out of the equation and setting my wife and kids up financially was a real option in my head—a thought that was more comforting than living.

I didn't have enough emotional intelligence to be a landlord. I was the wrong type of person to begin with, and in hindsight that is the biggest revelation. I was too rough around the edges—ready to fight for what I thought was right and emotionally challenged at the same time. Being a landlord, especially for the most needy in our society, isn't a good calling for someone like me. I believed they were who they said they were every time and would do the right thing if given the opportunity. They didn't.

Reliving these stories in order to write about them has brought back many bad memories. It's been very hard to walk back through some of this stuff, knowing that I did it wrong. I can't rewind the tape. I can't go back and be present when my kids were in school. It's tragic. Both of my children are well-balanced, productive adults, in spite of my being emotionally unavailable when in the grips of self-induced misery.

All of this took place a couple of hours south of Chicago. The laws in Illinois clearly favor the tenant, not the landlord. Laws, by the way, which were obviously made years ago by lawmakers who had never provided housing for anyone. Perhaps my experience would have been different in a different state. Maybe if I could have kicked someone out immediately instead of having to go through Illinois' expensive, outdated eviction process, it would have been better. Maybe if I had had more money and a team, I would have done better as well. But I was highly leveraged and paid more than I should have for the properties. Luckily, I had an excellent attorney that helped when I needed him most. Without him, I would have been left wide open for the cockroaches of our society to feed on. Even if I wanted to continue being a landlord, I wouldn't do it in Illinois, where mooching scumbags can live for free before being ordered to vacate.

The government housing in most cities is nicer than the old run-down houses that I owned. Those agencies get the best of the low-income crowd. The people left over are typically leftover for good reason. It could be because there isn't room in the nicer government units. Or it could be that they were kicked out of a nicer unit. I was dealing with people that had fallen through the cracks. People that didn't qualify for government assistance for whatever reason but still needed a place to live. I wanted to help all of them—right up until I realized they didn't care about me. Many were takers that weren't capable of giving anything, including basic respect and gratitude. The concept had never been introduced to them. Instead, they felt like shelter was a basic right.

Remember, I was a housing kid too. It was a different time in America though—the late seventies. A time when, maybe, there was still some dignity left in the world. My mother wasn't a lazy, bloated, loud-mouthed drug addict, pumping out multiple kids for welfare cash. Though uneducated, she was smart and resourceful. She was also responsible and put my brother and me first. She had escaped a bad marriage and needed a place to live which she could afford. Government-assisted housing was her only option at the time. She was grateful for it, held her head high, and made sure that it was temporary.

That is why I got the wires crossed in my head initially. I had hoped that my renters would be like my own mother. They weren't. My mother kept our house clean, kept us clean, kept herself clean. She didn't drink, do drugs, or smoke. She didn't allow us to be disrespectful. She didn't have a parade of men coming to our house either.

I thought that there would be several just like my mother that could benefit by dealing with an honest man that didn't want anything from them but rent. They weren't at all like my mother, however. I never met a tenant like her in all my years as a landlord, in spite of focusing on the best in everyone. I was searching for the soul of my mother in the eyes of some of the women that seemed so desperate, but never found it.

My father was a tenant for the last twenty years of his life. I remember him telling me a story about the New Year's Eve that his grandson ripped the thermostat off the wall in the old house he was renting. Around 11:00 p.m. he called his landlord, telling him he needed to come over and get the thermostat fixed.

I asked my dad why he called his landlord instead of trying to fix the problem himself. "That's his responsibility. That's what I pay him rent for," he said. I explained to my father that it wasn't his landlord's responsibility because he didn't cause the damage. Had it been me, I wouldn't have returned the phone call until the next day. My father didn't get it. At all.

His landlord did come on New Year's Eve and fixed the problem without any consequences for my father to experience. That was the landlord's mistake. He should have presented my father with a bill for the thermostat along with a bill for his time that was marked up for the holiday. But takers never see things that way. They always have a singular focus: themselves. Even my own father was oblivious. When you wreck a rental car, do you expect the rental car company to pay for the damages? Of course not. So when you are renting a home that is someone else's property, why is it so hard for people to understand that they are responsible for any damage they cause? It made me crazy.

The last couple of years as a landlord, I started carrying a gun. I enrolled in the concealed carry class, passed, and decided to carry a .40 cal Smith & Wesson with me everywhere, a bullet always loaded in the chamber. I had been threatened by some bad people that had nothing to lose. I wasn't looking for a fight but I wasn't going to let one more loser take advantage of me either. I was fed up with pimps, drug dealers, and unemployed wannabe gangsters. I stood my ground, didn't budge, didn't mince words or cower. After eight years in the trenches I wasn't about ready to give up. I was determined to see it all the way through and get as much of my money back as possible.

I'm not sure that the gun did anything other than give me peace of mind and enable me to conduct business without being scared for my life. I still have the Smith & Wesson but don't feel the need to carry it everywhere as I did then.

At least one of my former tenants is now homeless. I saw him last Thanksgiving Day, when my son and I were volunteering to serve on a breadline. This tenant, not mentioned in any of the stories, was bad news and I bounced him for instigating fights with neighbors and for not paying rent.

Now here we were at the breadline on Thanksgiving. The two of us made eye contact from across the crowded room. I had already wiped the debt away and forgotten about it. A Thanksgiving greeting would have been wonderful. Instead, he left immediately, without his free meal, avoiding an interaction.

I don't know what it's like to be him, but he must be carrying something so enormous and heavy that he can't deal with it. I tried hard to shoulder some of it for him when he was a tenant. He was an arrogant prick of a man who, like so many others, stiffed me out of money. So full of pride that it cost him literally *everything*. I fully understand why some people have to give up on their own blood to save themselves.

We all know that you cannot help someone who is unwilling to help himself. It is impossible and you can go broke trying. I learned to leave that role up to the government agencies that specialize in unlimited support for this segment of our society. Some of these tenants' bug in the rug mindsets were impenetrable. They were unwilling to peek their head out and see a whole new world full of opportunity and advancement. They were stuck in a cycle of poverty handed to them by their parents and generations before.

Character is the real measuring stick. I believe we are all more alike than we are different, and my belief includes every human being on earth. It's not limited to skin color, religion, or socioeconomic class. It's all about the content of our character. I knew I wasn't better than any of my tenants, at least not in the eyes of God. I later understood that the key separator is our choices. I had apparently made better choices. That is what it boiled down to.

My conclusion after ten years in the trenches was that most of my tenants were where they were in life for obvious reasons. Lack of education was the primary. Generational belief systems a strong second. Rarely was it about random circumstance, in spite of the hard luck victim stories I frequently heard. (Getting seriously ill can knock any of us on our ass, but not one of my tenants had a serious illness.)

A common theme with many of the bad tenants was their insatiable desire for instant gratification. They didn't wait *on* or *for* anything. There was no focus on a goal; there was no time spent thinking things through; there was no plan of any kind. They would simply wake up and start satisfying urges all day, like an animal. Delaying gratification wasn't even considered.

Many of these bad tenants were unemployed. They filled their brains with trashy programs displayed on giant flat screen televisions. They ate horrible food. Smoked and drank too much. Slept way more than they needed to. In some cases they drove cars they couldn't afford with monthly payments that were higher than their monthly rent. It was as if nothing in their life had been thought about for more than a few seconds.

Rick is an example. He had a nice car, a motorcycle, a really nice lawn tractor, which he didn't use, and a high-dollar drum set sitting in the living room of the house he rented from me. But Rick didn't have running water because he didn't pay his bill. He fell so far behind he couldn't get water restored until he paid the entire amount, which was hundreds of dollars. I didn't discover this until after he missed rent. He was bringing in five-gallon buckets of water from the neighbor's house, paying twenty dollars per bucket. That's four dollars per gallon. That's how stupid some of these people were. A gallon of gas was a dollar cheaper. Of course, he wanted me to "work with him" too. *Whatever, man, hit the bricks. I don't have time for it. Sell some of your shit, dumbass.*

I felt pushed further down into my self-created hell with every stupid-ass text or phone call from the takers:

"A burner on my oven doesn't work."
"I found what looks like a cockroach."
"The bathroom light is flickering."
"The neighbors are too loud."
"I didn't get my mail."
"I smell smoke."
"My bike got stolen."
"Can I pay half rent now and catch up next month?"
"Would you loan me twenty dollars?"
"Can I get a ride to the grocery store?"
"I want my roommate out."
"The sink is clogged."
"They didn't pick up my garbage."
"Can you shovel snow off my sidewalk?"

"The lawn looks burnt. You need to water it."
"Can we get some rock to fill in potholes in the driveway?"
"Can I have a cat?"
"Can I adopt a dog?"
"I want a new front door."
"Can I get a new fridge?"

It never stopped. How is it that normal self-sufficient people can live in a house for years without ever having a single issue?

My wife got mad at me for trying to make the homes too nice when I would renovate. She'd say, "These people don't care about anything. They are just going to trash it anyway, so quit trying so hard. You don't have to make it like something *we* would live in. Why buy the good stuff? Why spend extra money on nicer appliances? Why put in new carpeting? You are just throwing our money away." She was so right. I understand now why some landlords quit putting money back into their properties. I understand why they quit answering the phone too.

I learned to fix things. I had to. I didn't have the money to hire anyone, so I would just dive in. I rather liked fixing things and became quite handy. I had a deep sense of pride when I repaired an electric water heater on my own after watching a YouTube video. (Super easy by the way.)

My displeasure was never about the maintenance. It was always about the people. They were leeches, sucking the life right out of me. I started to *hate* them. They broke things often too. They'd break windows, doors, drawers, toilets, sinks, and anything else you can think of that is in a house. Then they would call me to come and fix it, making up a story about how "It was that way when I moved in," or "It just broke on its own." They were lying in every instance.

The homes of some of these renters stunk. They smelled like a mixture of fried food, body order, and cigarette smoke—a smell that I have associated with poverty my whole life, a smell that was embedded in the cash that many of these people paid their rent with. Their rent would stink up my whole car. I didn't dare bring the cash into our home. It smelled that bad.

In fact, I probably smelled like that when I was a teenager living with my father. He smoked and fried everything, and we were not as clean as we should have been. It was a source of shame for me as a kid and probably where I started forming some of my opinions. I bounced back and forth from my mother's home to my father's home in my early teens. My father didn't live in government housing, but his home wasn't as clean as my mother's.

Being poor doesn't mean you have to be dirty. It only means that you don't have a lot of resources in that moment. Lack of resources is temporary if you have the right attitude. There are steps that anyone in our society can take to get out of poverty.

Some of my worst tenants lived in disgusting filth. They didn't own a vacuum or toilet brush. They didn't use a toothbrush or have washrags. They didn't throw their trash away or wash their dishes. They let their laundry pile up on the floor. I felt sorry for some of them at first and even provided some basic necessities, until I learned that it wasn't because of lack. It was a choice. They knew better but didn't do better.

One of my tenants who didn't own a vacuum or pick up anything in his apartment found the money to purchase a massive two-thousand-dollar HDTV. I remember doing maintenance at his stinky home and walking past that beautiful television set. That was my proof that anyone could have whatever he focused on. Because whatever any of us focus on we are likely to get if we want it badly enough. This tenant simply hadn't set his sights any higher than a TV.

More than one tenant that I knew of was collecting disability benefits while simultaneously doing odd jobs for cash. And more than once, I was propositioned to "hire" someone on disability to do a job for cash. I was quick to point out that if they were able to work for cash, they shouldn't be on disability. No one liked to hear that truth of course. Scamming the government was fairly common among this group of people, and calling them on it was met with fierce defensiveness. I went off on one of these guys, telling him that he was a crook and I was going to report him.

A friend of mine once said, "You don't know what it's like to be one of them." My response was, *You're correct. I've been poor most of my life but I didn't let that define me. I didn't have anything handed to me. I have worked hard since I was twelve years old. I went to school. I graduated. I paid for most of my own living expenses as a teenager. I was working while my peers were at home with their families doing homework or enjoying themselves. I was working making tacos, while they were at the football games on Friday nights. I drove an old car I had purchased with paper route money. I started businesses, mowed lawns, and hustled my ass off chasing a career. Then I went back to college at age thirty-five and finished a degree—then paid every cent of that off too. You are correct, I don't know what it's like to be one of . . .* them!

Give me a damn break! I don't have time for people who sit on their ass, collect a check, and then turn right around and scam the same government that gave them the check.

People irritate me. I respect human life but I don't like most people. I look around and get angry. The lazy people that don't return the shopping carts or pick up the paper towel they dropped in a public bathroom, or people that merge in front of you in traffic at the last possible second. All of those people remind me of the worst of my tenants. Shitty, lazy, self-centered assholes. I have noticed that there are more and more of them every day too. Maybe their parents repeatedly told them that they were special and never got on their ass when they needed it most. Maybe they were never held accountable. Maybe no one has ever told them to pick up after themselves. I am not sure, but I know I rented to some really nasty people that were borderline animal and it changed my soul. I simply don't care about any of them any longer. I have had enough.

Slumlords have a bad reputation in our society. The slumlords in the movies, portrayed as mega wealthy, greedy, horrible people, are different than ones I met. I learned firsthand that the "slumlord persona" isn't real. The guys I met weren't billionaires. They didn't have *any* money, in fact. Many of us shared the same intent: to provide clean, well-kept rental housing for low-income tenants, making a little money along the way. Many were deeply in debt with no source of income other than their rental portfolio. I saw how hard they were working, how much money they spent, and they didn't have shit. Some wore rags for clothes and drove old vehicles that looked like they were going to fall apart at the next stop light. I could see the weariness in their face whenever we exchanged stories of takers. I watched as two of them lost everything they had trying to compete with major corporations and government agencies for tenants, and losing. I was paying attention.

The landlords that had money didn't buy the low-end stuff because they didn't want to deal with the low-end people. No, the landlords like me were barely getting by, stressed out, and angry. All had dealt with the lowest of the low just like me. One of them told me to "turn the keys into the bank and walk away."

Few people ever consider what the landlord goes through with careless, lying, destructive, dirty, nasty, rotten human beings. Yes, there are bad landlords out there too. Eventually, that is who the bad tenants are paired with, and I think that is destiny.

After a decade of hell, I sold all my properties for an amount that was less than what I had purchased them for, just to get rid of them. Selling them off at a discount stung, but it was worth it to have my life back. My loss was in the hundreds of thousands when you factor in unpaid rent, damages and improvements, legal fees, monthly expenses, and supplies.

I never factored in my time or assigned value to it. Yet I expected my employer to pay me thirty-five dollars per hour. How is that logical? Work for dirtbags for free—then expect an employer to pay you $35–$50 per hour. That was my biggest mistake because I will never get any of that time back. What would that total be anyway? Hundreds of thousands more? Was it ever worth it on any level? *No, not a chance in hell.*

I was incredibly happy the day the last property sold. It was blissful. It felt like being released from prison must feel for a person that was innocent the whole time. I didn't dread my phone ringing any longer either. I could breathe again. It was one of the happiest days of my life.

I had been in the business nine years and was planning my exit when I was given the opportunity to purchase one hundred units with seller financing and nothing down. I passed. (*Thank you, God!*) Sure, it's fun to think about collecting rent from one hundred units, but I knew the dark side well by that point. I knew how hard I had worked with twelve to fifteen units. One hundred more would only magnify my problems because the bad tenants in this space outnumbered the good ones ten to one. Plus I hadn't assembled a team. It was just me.

I could have filed bankruptcy twice but didn't. It would have been so much easier to turn the keys into the bank, file bankruptcy, then get back to my wife and kids. I never did. My credit rating plummeted (into the mid-six-hundred range) as I borrowed and borrowed to stay afloat. I dug my heels in and paid every single debt I owed. Part of that determination was out of spite, needing to prove to myself that I wasn't weak like the people that were taking advantage of me. The emotional toll this took on my family was enormous. I turned into a machine. Little to no joy and all work. My focus was on slaying the dragons. I succeeded but turned into a cold, nonsocial, uncaring man in the process.

I had some great tenants too. They were wonderful because they were kind, paid their rent on time, and didn't ever make *their* problems *my* problems. Just because they didn't have any money didn't mean they were bad people. Being poor isn't a sin. Being a self-centered asshole is.

In addition to some hard-learned lessons, there were some pure blessings along the way.

Blessings Along the Way

The best tenants are the ones you never hear from. They are busy living their lives and let you live yours. They aren't needy. They don't pry. They pay their rent and don't cause problems with anyone. By the grace of God, I was fortunate enough to have some good tenants. What they lacked in money they compensated for with character. They were the blessings along the way that made the experience worth seeing through to the end. Had I done a better job vetting my tenants and being patient, it's likely I would have encountered more of these good people and my experience would have been dramatically different.

Ernie, from an earlier chapter, was a retired painter and veteran. He was funny and we made me each other laugh. He always paid his rent on time and didn't ask for anything. If he broke something he fixed it. Because he had been living in the building for over ten years when I purchased it, I kept his rent unusually low. It was worth it to me to keep him happy. He loved the little apartment and was a bother to no one. I considered him a friend. When he started slipping away mentally, his children's intervening was something I really appreciated.

Tina as well was a great tenant—a single mom who had been a teenager when she birthed her son. He was in his late teens when I met them. Tina's remarkable honesty was refreshing. She was humble to the point that I had to pump her up every now and then, reminding her of her own value. Life hadn't been easy for her. Years ago Tina's grandmother had lived in the same home, so she had childhood memories of the small place, which she loved. She kept it spotless and took care of the property, going so far as to make upgrades (a new window or new appliance) with her own money. Always considerate, she'd ask before starting and I would let her, discounting the rent in the amount of the upgrade. Wonderful and fair, she wasn't a taker. I had visions of handing her the keys to the house, telling her that she owned it now and didn't have to pay me a thing. But, of course, I couldn't do that, because I owed so much on it myself.

Another noteworthy tenant was Russell. He was close to seventy years old when I purchased the house he was living in from another investor. He chain smoked and drank Natural Light by the case, but he was a good guy. Always happy. His best friends were his ex-wife and her new husband. Sometimes he'd stay with them for the weekend. That's the type of guy he was. He always paid his rent on time and even tried to help me out by watching the building I owned that was right next to his house. He'd offer to help the other tenants too—unloading groceries or maybe scooping snow off a sidewalk. He wasn't at all a taker; instead, he'd put something back into the bucket every day, even if simply a smile or words of encouragement. If all the tenants were half as good as this old veteran, I would still be in the game. Sadly, people like him are fewer and fewer.

I still believe there is good in all of us. I make no apologies for how I feel about any of these people. I gave each of them an honest chance, and they ruined it. Sure, there are likely contributing factors that I know nothing about. Sure, some of the circumstances may have been beyond their control at the time. But it was a business for me, not a charity. I was the *blessing* that some of these poor souls needed at the time. But they couldn't see it for what it was, too busy drowning in the consequences of their bad choices.

I had an excellent business relationship with a local small-town banker, now vice president and slated to be president. We are still in contact today. His bank holds the mortgage on my home. He knew I was struggling as a landlord at different points but never pressured me. Instead he helped me, knowing my word was good. He waited for me to get caught up when he didn't have to. He and the board at the bank took a big chance on me, and it paid off. I made good. I never had the intention of leaving them high and dry—that isn't part of my make-up. Having them in the trenches with me made all the difference.

My insurance agent was also wonderful. He offered his assistance whenever he could and it was genuine. Total class. One night when one of my tenants threw flour on a furnace fire (*yeah?*), he offered to help me get things cleaned up and in order. He insisted that I let him come but I refused, telling him that I would handle it—partly because the neighborhood was a little rough that time of night and I knew I had a drug dealer living close by. I didn't want to put this "good neighbor" in harm's way. I had called him to initiate a claim but didn't end up filing one. I am still a fan of his today—a solid guy that has never stopped doing good things for others.

My mother-in-law helped too, loaning me some cash when the bottom dropped out and it was tax time. No questions asked. She simply wrote out a check and said, "Pay me when you can." The day I sold the last house I went straight to her home and handed her a cashier's check, interest included. She never had much of anything, and it made me feel guilty taking money from her in the first place. As a way to help her, I had purchased a run-down piece of property of hers. That was the house that I needed to pay taxes on and she helped me. I am confident that she has a place reserved in heaven.

December 2018 my father passed. We had a stressed relationship my whole life, but I loved him. There were some great things about him. One was how he could light up a room with his sense of humor. Another was that he paid his rent on time. He used to tell me, "Pay your rent first, son. You will always need a roof over your head." Another piece of advice was for me to *Stay where the money is and you won't have any problems*. He was referring to staying out of bad areas of Chicago but it applies to all cities, I suppose. He was correct in saying that I should have stayed out of those areas. I didn't listen though. I spent ten years trying to make a bag of shit smell better. Another piece of wisdom that he offered was that *You can't make sense out of no sense*. I often wondered if that was from a movie he had seen. If not, I think it speaks volumes and I love it. Thanks, Dad. You did have value, even if you could never see it yourself.

My brother and his family live on the West Coast and are doing amazingly well. My mother lives in downstate Illinois, and she too is enjoying a comfortable life, as she should be. She still does volunteer work for others and will likely do that sort of thing until she no longer can.

My family was a true blessing. My wife never gave up on me. She knew I had made some really bad decisions but didn't rub it in my face. She could have easily left, taking the kids with her. We had experienced some rough patches before all of this anyway. Instead, she did an amazing job nurturing our children and keeping our home clean and safe. Proof of that can be seen today in how well adapted and productive both of our kids are. Neither my daughter nor son is a taker. They have respect for other people's property, and both pay their rent on time, every time. I have claimed my shortcomings and offered a heartfelt apology for my words and actions when at my worst. I am so incredibly thankful that I got rid of all the properties and the problems associated with them, so I could get back to having fun and making positive memories with my family.

There are many more that I could mention. Thank you to all who helped along the way. You know who you are. I love you for it.

Advice for Tenants and Landlords

Being a good tenant is really simple:

1. Pay your rent on time.
2. Keep the property clean and take care of it.
3. Don't make your problems the landlord's problems.

More Advice for Being a Good Tenant

Mind your own business.
Retain renter's insurance.
Don't be a pain.
Fix what you break.
Don't lie.
Don't let people live with you unless they are on the lease.
Don't hide from responsibility.
Don't expect the landlord to remodel the place.
Don't rent a place you don't like.
Check the landlord out. See if he or she has been sued. Ask other tenants.
Treat your landlord with respect.
Don't call after regular business hours.
Don't create emergencies that really aren't emergencies.
Don't alter anything in the unit without permission.

Don't paint any walls, floors, doors, etc.
Don't assume the landlord owes you anything.
Read your lease. No excuses.
Be kind to your neighbors.
No Pets means no pets.
No Smoking means no smoking.
Don't be stupid.

Advice for Landlords

Either get all of the rent and deposit up front, or say no.
Enforce the lease.
Don't look the other way. Report abusive behavior to authorities.
Don't let anyone live in a unit unless they are on the lease.
Don't listen to excuses about late rent.
Do a walk through before you hand the tenant the keys. Get a signature at the bottom.
Don't offer to fix anything that a tenant breaks.
Don't refund the deposit unless the place is as good or better than when you rented it.
Don't allow tenants to bother you outside business hours.
Define what an emergency is. (*Blood, flood, or power*—all else can wait until the morning.)
Don't answer calls from bad tenants. Let them leave voice mail or text messages.
Don't waste your time with idiots.
Treat everyone with dignity, but remain firm.
Don't make exceptions, ever.
Take photos of the unit *before* and *after* a tenant rents from you. Keep records.
Charge tenants for lockouts.

Charge tenants for late rent.
Charge tenants for the application, to cover your costs.
Run a background check on every tenant.
Trust your gut and say no if you feel you should.
Never discriminate based on ethnicity.
The Golden Rule applies.

About the Author

Max Bumgardner quickly became overwhelmed trying to build a real estate portfolio comprised of low-end housing units. As a child he lived in government-assisted housing with his single mother and brother; as an adult he became what some would term a slumlord. He stayed in that role for over ten years. Max started his foray into landlording after a successful twenty-five-year career as a morning radio host. He is the father of two adult children and lives with his wife in Illinois.

If you have a story that you would like to share about a landlord or tenant, please contact Max at slumlordstories@gmail.com.